LONG
STORY
SHORT

LONG STORY SHORT

THE BIBLE IN SIX SIMPLE MOVEMENTS

JOSHUA McNALL

Seedbed

Scripture quotations are taken from the Holy Bible, New International Version®,
NIV® Copyright © 1973, 1978, 1984, 2011 by Biblica, Inc.™ Used by permission
of Zondervan. All rights reserved worldwide. www.zondervan.com The "NIV"
and "New International Version" are trademarks registered in the United States
Patent and Trademark Office by Biblica, Inc.™ All rights reserved worldwide.

Printed in the United States of America

Cover design by Micah Kandros
Page design by PerfecType, Nashville, Tennessee

McNall, Joshua.
  Long story short : the Bible in six simple movements / Joshua McNall. –
Franklin, Tennessee : Seedbed Publishing, ©2018.

     pages ; cm. + 1 videodisc.

     ISBN 9781628245875 (paperback)
     ISBN 9781628245967 (DVD)
     ISBN 9781628245882 (Mobi)
     ISBN 9781628245899 (ePub)
     ISBN 9781628245905 (uPDF)

     1. Theology, Doctrinal--Popular works. 2. Bible--Theology--Popular works.
     I. Title. II. Series.

BT77.M362 2018   230/.41   2018955414

 Seedbed

SEEDBED PUBLISHING
Franklin, Tennessee
seedbed.com

For my father, Greg McNall

CONTENTS

PREFACE

Whatever you do, don't make it more academic!" This helpful statement was the only firm advice given by the folks at Seedbed as we first talked about revising and releasing the book that you now hold. I wrote much of it more than a decade ago for the people of my home church near Grand Rapids, Michigan. At the time, I was a young pastor fresh out of seminary, with no kids, and a full head of hair. Now I am a theology professor with four children and a bald spot caused by every aspect of this sentence. I love how life has changed for my wife, Brianna, and me in the past decade! Yet some of those changes have introduced the danger of taking something simple and making it too "academic."

I've tried to fight that impulse like the plague.

While this is a book about the Bible, it is *not* a book for scholars. In fact, if you are one of those, you should probably put it down right now. You will not like it. Instead, this is a book for all those regular folks for whom the Bible seems daunting or confusing. It is for all those people who have ever tried to understand the Scriptures but found the Bible intimidating, strange, or even offensive.

I've been there. In fact, some of us are scholars now because that strangeness lodged itself inside of us—like a fire in our bones. As a teenager, I rode home from church

...amp each summer with a resolution etched within my mind (and probably within my hipster Moleskin journal). Amidst the camp speaker's annual challenge to remain pure, witness to the heathen football team, and avoid Metallica like my very soul depended on it, I would make myself a promise: *This year I will read my Bible! This year will be different! This year, I will start each morning in God's Word. I'll start in Genesis!*

And each year, near Leviticus, I'd fail.

Ever been there?

As a pastor's kid, I should have had an advantage in the Bible department. After all, I knew many parts by heart. Yet while I knew the stories of people like David, Samson, or Solomon, I didn't know the Big Story in which all those little narratives fit together. As I note later, it was a bit like having all the pieces to a puzzle without the glossy picture on the box top. My ignorance was no one's fault. But for whatever reason, the Bible struck me as mostly a collection of lessons or rules by which to live.

In the words of a terrible Christian song from the late '90s, it was the B.I.B.L.E.—"Basic Instructions Before Leaving Earth." As for such instructions, there was David on sexual (im)purity; the book of Acts for evangelizing the heathens (read: football players); and there were even some demon stories to rule out Metallica.

What more could you need?

Turns out, a lot.

While I've hardly had all my Bible questions answered over the years (sometimes I've just got new questions), I have been convinced that glimpsing the big picture of God's Story can help all the little stories make more sense. Here's the one and only big idea for this book: when understood as a single plotline from beginning to end, Scripture comes alive, not just as rules or lessons, but as an unfolding drama that sucks us into the performance. As a story, it is without peer in all of human history. In fact, the Story *is* all of human history. It begins with creation and crescendos to a new creation that comes to heal our mess of sin and death.

In an age of biblical illiteracy (or sheer boredom), my goal is to take the Bible from a closed book to an open one. My approach, however, is not to fill your head with more information, but to awaken your imagination to the beauty of God's grand drama. In terms of content, this book introduces the Scriptures not as a complex list of rules or doctrines, but as a single Story—a script—in six simple movements: creation, the fall, Israel, Jesus, the church, and the new creation.

With this narrative in place, the reader will then (hopefully) begin to understand how all the little stories of the Bible fit together into a seamless whole. And what's more important, you will be compelled to step into the drama as a part of its performance.

At the end of each chapter, you'll find two things meant to help you: First, there will be a selection of Bible passages that you may want to read for yourself, to actually engage with the Story we've been sketching. Second, there will be some discussion questions that can be used to go deeper in a community. This type of relational reading is important, because as I argue, God's Story emerges *from* and *for* community. That is, human history itself comes forth *from* and *for* relationships of holy love (more on that in chapter 1).

ACKNOWLEDGMENTS

My life has been blessed with many meaningful relationships. Thanks go first to my parents, Greg and Bonita McNall, who taught me about Jesus and his love. It was not their fault that I struggled to read the Bible for so long. Rather it was their "fault" that I wanted to read it at all. The original manuscript for this book was dedicated to my dad—and so is this one. The reason is a simple one: some men write better stories with their lives than can be published with word processors. I love you, Dad.

Thanks go also to my teachers. I've been blessed, over the years, to learn from some fantastic educators, whether in college, seminary, or PhD work. Such relationships have shown me yet another reason Jesus was called "Rabbi." Teachers matter. And in my own life, these men and women helped ignite in me a love of learning, reading, and good questions. So while any errors in this volume are mine alone, the book would not exist without my "Rabbis."

In the notes, there are pointers to more detailed sources that have helped me over the years. The Bible scholar N. T. Wright bulks large among these resources. As do others for whom "academic" is not a shame word.

Thanks also to my good friend Chad McCallum (the would-be "stand-up comedian" from chapter 5).

I was serving under Chad's leadership as his assistant pastor when I first wrote these chapters. Among other things, he showed me that ministry can be fun as well as faithful, and that humor can be a conduit to the Christlike transformation.

Finally, my deepest (earthly) debt of love goes to Brianna. She is a better wife than I could have ever hoped for; and I'm thankful every day that I asked her to marry me. We were just newlyweds when I first wrote this book. Now we have four children, who, in their best aspects, take after her: Lucy, Penelope, Ewan, and Teddy. Dad loves you kids too! I hope that someday you read this book and catch a glimpse of God's Father-love that puts even mine to shame.

Now, without any further ado, let me tell you a story.

LONG

STORY

SHORT

INTRODUCTION

Why You Should Stop Reading

I've been told by people older and wiser than myself that the purpose of writing a proper introduction is to convince more finicky readers that they should in fact *keep reading*. This is important. I am supposed to grab you by the collar and convince you that somewhere, perhaps on the bottom of page 137, there is an insight so profound that it will simultaneously bless your soul, cure your psoriasis, and reverse male pattern baldness.

Let me be clear: there is no magic insight. Still, I tried at first to write that kind of introduction. I tried to *sell it*. But in the end, I always came off feeling like the old guy on those late-night infomercials—the one with the spray tan—who sells electric food dehydrators. "This book will revolutionize your life!" I'd say. "Now taste the beef jerky!"

So rather than tell you why you should keep reading, let's say we take the opposite approach. Imagine (for a moment) that you've *stopped* reading. That's right.

Envision for a second that someone waved an old-fashioned pocket watch in front of your face and uttered a cheesy hypnotic phrase with the inflection of a yoga teacher: "You are not reading . . . there are no words; no letters; no pages pinched between your fingertips. You are not reading. *You* are *walking*."

Imagine now that you are walking between the towering shelves of an ancient library. Where you come from, libraries are not exactly places to write home about. But this space is different. The room is incredible. It's the kind of space that camera-toting tourists pay five bucks apiece to gawk at; or in which you might expect to see a sign for the "Hogwarts Reunion, Class of 1998." Above you, shafts of natural light spill in through the colored glass of gothic windows. Overhead, the vaulted ceilings remind you of cathedrals you have seen in pictures. But this is not a house of worship. At least not now. The building itself seems centuries old, but the books seem even older. As you walk between the wooden shelves, bound pages smell of mildew and far-off places.

Then as you are walking, suddenly your eye is caught by a single spine from a single volume. On the surface, there is no reason to notice this book more than others. There is nothing extraordinary about its size or color. Still it catches your attention. After pausing for a moment, you stretch on tiptoes to retrieve the dusty volume. You grasp it, turn it over, and scan the front for some kind of title. Nothing. There's no proper introduction, either.

What you find instead, inside the tattered binding, is something else entirely. There, tucked inside the leather cover is what appears to be a kind of label. It simply reads: *The Book*.

"The Book?" you ask.

It is, you suppose, an accurate description. But couldn't the author be just a bit more specific. After all, how did he expect to *sell it*? The whole thing seems strange. Then again, being somewhat strange yourself, you make a snap decision. You tuck the mystery book under your arm and proceed to check it out.

Now you *are* reading.

In a Starbucks around the corner, you leaf through the tattered pages. *What is this thing?* you wonder. But the reading hardly eliminates the questions. Between the moth-eaten covers is an odd assortment of poems, biographies, genealogies, and legal minutia, all *smooshed* together in a single binding. The variety suggests that this is actually a *combination* of several books—with different authors, agendas, and historical contexts. It's a hodge-podge. It's a mash-up. And while some parts are understandable enough, others are downright baffling. Still, it does have all the stuff that makes for a good movie: violence, sex, even a talking animal near the beginning.

Later, however, as you begin to spend more time within the musty pages, you begin to perceive what one could not have noticed at first glance. Despite different topics and styles of writing, you begin to glimpse what appears to be a *single story* running through the pages, like a river through the forest. This plotline is like a long, thin thread that ties all the parts together: a single narrative. It is illumined in different ways, to be sure, by different authors, and through different genres, but it is visible nonetheless. There is a single history from beginning to end. It takes some time to see it, but it is there—a story—from start to finish.

As in all great stories, there is a beginning. There are key characters. There are false hopes, foils, twists of plot, and twists of fate. There is a climax. There is a hero. And as with all great stories, there is an ending which both *does* and *does not* bring the resolution you've been waiting for. Were they leaving room for a final installment? And it is now that a peculiar realization hits you: perhaps this is a book worth reading.

Now stop imagining.

The Book

Everything that follows is an attempt to answer just one question: *What if the Christian Scriptures are a bit like this imaginary volume in this imaginary library?*

Literally translated, "the Bible" simply means "the books."[1] That's it. We may wish it were something more profound or creative, but it's not. The Bible is first and foremost a collection of different books, written by different authors, in a time and culture immensely different from our own. The Bible is different. And, in the end, all these differences lead us to an inevitable conclusion: when compared to almost everything else we read—from *Rolling Stone* to *Robinson Crusoe*—the Bible is rather odd.

The Bible is strange. We avoid saying such things in the hope of sounding smart or respectful, but it doesn't change the fact. The book is an anomaly in our modern world. It is published and purchased like clockwork, but it is read and understood more rarely. The Scriptures have a foreignness about them. They have an ancient quality that draws us, convicts us, and then leaves us with questions. The Bible is different. And if it doesn't strike you that way, then it may be because you haven't taken time to really read it. Don't think so? Try starting in the Old Testament book of Judges. That should do the trick.

The Bible is also challenging. And for this reason, much ink is spilled each year in an effort to take what it actually *says* and transform it into something more palatable to our modern taste buds. We like practical insights and seven-step formulas. As a local radio station touts, we like "positive and encouraging hits—safe for the whole family." We like greeting cards, so we turn the Bible into one.

But consider for a moment if all this well-intentioned *distilling* and *formulizing* were actually having an unintended consequence. Imagine if by constantly analyzing the individual pieces of the jigsaw puzzle we somehow forgot to take a look at the beautiful picture on the front of the box.[2]

To be blunt, that is precisely what sometimes happens in the church. A brief trip to any Christian bookstore will reveal dozens of studies on particular *topics* within the Bible. You can read about marriage, dating, finances, spiritual gifts, even biblical dieting (whatever that is).

There are also dozens of helpful studies on specific *texts* within the Bible. You can do a study on the book of James or John or Acts. But aside from all these topical and textual studies, there are fewer resources that provide a snapshot of the big picture on the front of the box. There are fewer resources available that give a simple telling of the plotline from beginning to end. The book I've written is not for scholars. And while I am an academic, my hope is that you will not notice that too much while reading. It is a book for the church, just as the Bible is. It is for people who find the Bible confusing, strange, or even scary. It is a book for those students in my New Testament classes who have never read the Scriptures, and who need some help believing that they should even try. This book is for you. It is a glimpse of God's long Story (in the Scriptures) made short—or at least shorter.

Thankfully, the Bible is *not* primarily a collection of disembodied truths. It is not primarily a cosmic rule book, an anthology of practical insights, or a five-step path toward psychological fulfillment. The Bible is primarily a story—and it reveals for us the remarkable narrative of God's work within our world.

Our question then is simple: What are the basic *chapters* in this plotline? What are the basic stages in the drama? What are the essential twists and turns? And why should these details matter to any of us?

Why Bother?

This last question is the most important one. Why should the narrative of the Bible matter to anyone today? Why bother with people and places whose names are all but impossible to pronounce? I mean really, Jehoshaphat?

Why not stick with our formulas, our simple lists of dos and don'ts, and our prepackaged devotional insights? Why bother delving into the violent and murky memories of ancient history? "Enough with the minutia!" you say. "Get to the point!"

Fair enough.

The point is simple. The biblical plotline ought to matter to us because we all play a part in it, whether we like it or not. We ought to know the Big Story of Scripture because whether we are aware of it or not, we are living in a chapter of that Story now. We inhabit it— with people whose names and hometowns we know well. We need to know the overarching narrative of Scripture because *this Story* is *our story*. And to live wisely in our chapter, we must know the chapters that precede and follow our own.

To use a metaphor from the theater: if we are to know how to act in this scene, we must know the scenes that have come before. To play our part in God's drama, we must know how the plot has unfolded up to now. And we must know how the play will end. Is it comedy or tragedy? Who is the hero? Who is the villain? In short: if we are to act well, we must know the script—and the script is Scripture.[3]

The answer to the why is, therefore, not that complicated: we must know the story of Scripture because we are all characters in it. We can be heroes or villains, mere extras or key players, good or bad actors. We must know the story because it is the story of human history—it is our story—and we have a share in how it ends.

Chapters in the Plotline

To get to know the Story we are part of, we will break down the biblical narrative into six chapters.

We'll start in the beginning with creation. We'll move second to what Christians call the fall. (The Story takes a nasty turn here.) We'll spend a third chapter exploring the beginning of God's rescue operation through a people called Israel. Then, we'll see the rescue climax in a person named Jesus. Next, we'll discover what it means to follow Jesus as part of his church. And, finally, we'll see how the Story comes full circle—and then some—in a beautiful and surprising event called the new creation.[4]

These chapters will constitute our plotline—God's long Story made short. And for those who like their ideas in bullet points, here they are again:

- Creation
- Fall
- Israel
- Jesus
- Church
- New Creation

It's not important if these headings mean little to you now. Think of this as merely a table of contents. Each chapter indicates a different scene within the human drama, but they are all connected. No part of the play will make much sense without the others. Incidentally, this may be one reason why the Bible has failed to connect with you in the past. Without glimpsing the big picture on the front of the box, it is difficult to see how the little pieces fit together.

Likewise, when you begin to grasp how these stages in the drama come together, you may find that the strange parts of Scripture make more sense. (Not entirely, mind you, since all great tales resist our taming.) And, in reading, you may find that some religious assumptions that you've held for years actually have little to do with God's Story. And you may find that you are able to open the Bible to almost any place and know quite quickly which chapter you are reading. You will begin to grasp why God did something way back then, and why it has ramifications for us now.

And, most important, you may begin to see God more clearly for who he really is. He is not merely a cosmic school master handing down rules and regulations. He is not the divine equivalent of a motivational speaker, peddling buttery inspiration like *Chicken Soup for the Soul*. He is not a heavenly Santa Claus, a spiritual buddy, or a complete mystery that seeks only to baffle us.

God is more. He is an artist, a creator, and in many ways, a writer. He is the composer of the most beautiful and terrible love story that the world has ever known. In its own way, the Bible is Shakespeare with soul. It is Homer on truth serum. It is Hemingway shot through with hope. In its pages, we glimpse the Big Story of human history, and with each passing second, we move closer to the final chapter. This is God as Writer-Redeemer, the author of history who steps into the plotline to rescue the tale from sure disaster. *This* is a God worth paying attention to. Yet we glimpse this

Creator-God only when we begin to find in the ancient words of our mysterious *book* the most incredible script to have ever been penned. The script is Scripture; it's God's Story, and it's worth reading.

CREATION

Why Sugar Momma Had to Die

Back in my school days, I read a story about some people in a place called Babylon. It was a tale about creation, and it explained how this ancient culture believed that the earth, the universe, and human beings all came to be.

It started with a *fight*.

According to the Babylonians, the struggle was between the gods. I couldn't help but notice that it ended like a lot of human fights I've seen. That is, it ended in a bloody mess. In this creation story, there were two main characters: one called Tiamat (I will refer to her as "Sugar Momma") and another called Marduk. Tiamat was a mother goddess, and she had a son named Kingu.

The story didn't say so, but apparently Kingu was an only child because his mother liked to dote on him even more than usual. She liked it so much, in fact, that one day Sugar Momma went so far as to name her golden boy as the undisputed boss of all the other deities. Stop me if you've heard this one before. She even held a ceremony. Picture an over-the-top suburban sweet sixteen.

Unfortunately, as it often does with spoiled children, the parental favoritism didn't sit too well with all the other gods. They didn't like Kingu. They thought he was a punk. And they decided to do something. After some heated discussion, a rival god was chosen. He would face Tiamat and he would tell Sugar Momma to stop playing favorites, or else. The rival god they found was Marduk. Cue the *Rocky* theme music.

Trouble ensued.

In what sounds like a Babylonian royal rumble, there was a showdown between the deities. They fought, and it was messy. As the story goes, at the end of the brawl both Sugar Momma and her golden boy lay dead. But in case you thought that was the end, it's not. Things were just getting interesting. (Remember, the story is about *creation*.) After Marduk murdered his rivals, he wasn't finished with them. In a gory fit of creativity, he decided to *make something* from the remains of his slain foes. According to the Babylonians, he created the earth from the mangled scraps of Tiamat, and human beings from the bloody corpse of Kingu.[1] Somewhere, Quentin Tarantino proclaimed that "it was good."

Creation from Conflict

This may seem like an odd way to begin a chapter on creation, but upon reading this grotesque old story I had a slightly different reaction than you might expect. That is, I thought it sounded pretty normal. Because, in some ways, conflict is a pretty standard description of the way it goes when new things are created. Stay with me. What I mean is, when you think about it, creativity is almost always *fueled* by struggle, adversity, suffering, and tension.

It's that way in business. Two executives disagree about the best way to make an app (or whatever). Trouble ensues. Things get tense. And before long one person decides to go on her own and do things differently. A new company is born, and new products flood the market. It's creation, from conflict.

It's that way with nations too. Country A passes a law that says certain people far away have to pay high taxes on their tea. Certain people are *not* pleased. In fact, some folks actually go so far as to throw said tea into the local harbor. Trouble ensues. Things get tense. And, before you know it, there are two countries where there used to be one. It's creation, from conflict. (Word to the wise: never mess with people's tea.)

It's that way in music too. A young and talented musician feels that his parents' music fails to connect with the way he sees the world. It hems him in. It's too restrictive. A struggle ensues, and in a fit of creativity, Young and Talented Musician grabs an instrument and breaks all the rules. (I'm referring of course to Mozart. Or maybe Kurt Cobain. Or any musician that really matters.) It's creation out of conflict.

The same principle holds true in science and sports, art and architecture, and pretty much everything in between. Creation is almost always *fueled* by conflict.

This is especially true when we begin to study the various creation stories floating around the ancient and modern world. Biblical scholars tell us that perhaps the *most unique* element of the Jewish-Christian account of origins is its complete and utter lack of conflict. There are other unique features, of course. But this one really sets our narrative apart. Virtually every other ancient (or modern) creation story involves some sort of violent or sexual conflict.

Consider also the big bang theory—at least when it is divorced from some benevolent oversight. To put it crudely, scientists tell us that the bang is merely a metaphor used to describe an intense reaction that occurred when multiple cosmic gases, well . . . interacted violently. As the story goes, the gasses conflicted, reacted, and *bang*! The universe was made (much like Tiamat and golden boy's remains).

Come to think of it, maybe the Babylonian story isn't as unique as one might think. (At least, minus the particulars about divine disembowelment.) If we are honest, it sometimes seems that violence has been stitched into the eternal fabric of the universe. It governs the animal kingdom and it blankets the cable news networks. Nature, as they say, is "red in tooth and claw." Tarantino has reason to be smiling.

Creation from and for Communion

So what would a more *original* creation story look like? Where would it begin if not with conflict? Well, if you believe the Scriptures, a more original story of creation would start with something many of us have only experienced in passing. A truly original story of creation would start with perfect, loving community. Now *that* would be subversive.

The creation chapter in *God's Story* is an attempt to open our minds to the possibility that there is indeed another story out there—a more beautiful story—and one that rings truer. We find it in the Scriptures. What we discover, when we read the Bible carefully, is that the universe emerges not from violent or sexual conflict, not from the clash of volatile personalities or volatile gases, but *from* and *for* community.

In the Bible, everything from anteaters to jellyfish, waterfalls to water buffaloes, sunsets to supernovas—*everything* emerges *from* and *for* persons in loving relationship. This is the classic Christian doctrine of creation. But it is also the doctrine of the Trinity. Our universe came into being *from* a God who *is* communion (Father, Son, and Spirit). And it emerges *for* persons (both divine and human) who will live together with that same concern for one another. This is the picture of creation that we'll be examining. But first, to more weighty matters.

In the Refrigerator

Few know it, but I was recently diagnosed with a fairly serious medical condition. There is probably a fancy Latin name for it, but the reality is that I am a chronic *loser*. That's right. I have a condition that forces me to lose things, especially car keys—and as far as I can tell, there is no cure.

Because of this obscure condition, I have been required, like some of you, to develop a kind of search-and-rescue procedure that kicks in whenever I leave home. It's basically a protocol that covers all the places that I typically set down the car keys. I start with the one place they are supposed to be: the key hook by the door. *After all*, I think, *we put that hook there for a purpose*. It would make sense for them to be there. It's logical. But they aren't. They never are.

So I proceed next to a number of other logical locations. I check the dresser, the counter, the sofa, the pocket of a discarded pair of pants. And sometimes this yields results. But sometimes it doesn't. Because I have a *condition*.

And it's in such instances that I am forced to get more creative. I was in one of these situations the other day when I remembered something that gave me hope. I remembered my sandwich. More specifically, I remembered *making* my sandwich, which required mayonnaise. And because my wife, Brianna, isn't fond of food poisoning, we usually keep the mayonnaise in the fridge. So it was, in the end, that I opened the refrigerator to find what I had been searching for: my car keys, between the bologna and the carrot sticks.

Beginning an exploration of creation by looking to the Old Testament book of Job (pronounced: "Jobe") may seem as wise as beginning a search for the car keys by looking in the refrigerator. Why go there? Yet in the Scriptures, as in life, we sometimes find what we're looking for in the strangest of places. In Job's world, creation and community have been shattered. His life has been rocked by events beyond his control. And he is the victim of suffering that he did not bring upon himself. Without warning, his universe is torn apart by sickness, death, fair-weather friends, a natural disaster—and if all that isn't bad enough—a nagging wife who wants him dead.[2] It's a bad day.

Yet what God gives Job in the middle of all this pain is not at all what we'd expect. He doesn't give him a philosophical answer to the problem of evil—not at all. He doesn't tell Job *why* bad things happen. He doesn't even bend down to whisper that God loves him and has a wonderful plan for his life. Instead, what God gives to Job in his moment of need is an oratorical slap in the face, accompanied by a dizzying picture of *creation*. It's strange. In Job's moment of deep personal tragedy, the Creator sidesteps words of comfort, and instead launches immediately into an ear-splitting retelling of the first chapter in the Bible's plotline. Why is that?

Singing Stars and Shouting Angels

When we pick up the episode, Job is loudly questioning the justice of God. "Something must be wrong up there!" he screams. "I've done nothing to deserve all this!" (And he's correct.) Still it's not Job's question, but God's response, that startles us. Instead of comforting Job with a warm embrace or a cold beer, God asks him a question, and it's a pointed one: *Where were you? Where were you, Job, when I created all of this? Surely you can tell me! What were you doing on the day I formed the universe? Where were you?* (To be honest, this is a little like asking most of us where we were the last time the Whig party won the White House. Answer: Uh . . . I wasn't.) God asks Job this question but he doesn't even give him time to answer. Instead, he paints Job a picture, and tells him a story. It's a picture of creation and a story of communal celebration.

In a moment of anger and suffering, God grasps Job by the collar and gives him the only thing that will quiet him long enough to trust him through the pain. It's not a greeting card cliché or a Sunday school answer. It's a ringside seat to the bowel-shaking formation of the heavens and the earth.

In a free-verse poetic smackdown, God gives Job a whirlwind tour of how he crafted the most intricate features of the cosmos. He tells him how he subdued the seas, hung the heavens, counted clouds, and on and on it goes. It is beautiful, frightening, awe-inspiring stuff. Shakespeare would salivate. You should read it.

And right in the middle of these poetic verses, there is one line that tells us something about the context out of which our story begins. It is a brief line, not even a full sentence, but it reveals for us a scene of celebration and community that lies at the very heart of the universe. Here, God explains to Job that while he effortlessly set the galaxies to spinning, something else was happening too. *He wasn't alone.* Rather, at the very moment of unveiling: "the morning stars sang together and all the angels shouted for joy" (Job 38:7).

If this verse strikes us as strange, it may be because when we picture God creating the heavens and the earth (if we even can), we sometimes picture a solitary old man with a beard—who may or may not sound like Morgan Freeman—calling people and animals into being so that he can have someone to hang out with. Maybe God was lonely, we think, so he made us. But the Scriptures tell a different story: In the Scriptures, it is not creation out of loneliness, or creation out of conflict. In the Scriptures, it is always creation from community. It's creation as a *party*. Stars sing in harmony. Angels shout for joy. It's a raucous affair.

Of course, we could easily dismiss such words as mere poetic metaphors. "After all," says Captain Obvious, "stars don't sing." Perhaps not. But even metaphors are meant to point at truth.

God is saying something to Job, and it is something unique among the dozens of other creation stories in the world. To a man whose life is fractured and fragmented, God delivers a clear message. *The story doesn't start that way!* The story starts with perfect, beautiful community.

Perhaps you need to hear that too. The story of creation is not the tale of a lonely deity looking for companionship. God wasn't gloomily reading the personal ads when he crafted the galaxies. Creation is not the tale of a friendless old man who made the universe because he needed some people to talk to. Nor is it the violent story of angry gods and goddesses fighting and fornicating for control of the cosmos. It didn't happen by accident. Creation is the story of an Artist effort-lessly sculpting the universe amid a chorus of thankful celebration. The universe was born amid a party: stars singing, angels shouting. It was the opposite of violent conflict. It was creation *from* community.

Such party imagery also points to another crucial truth: the unabashed goodness of the (physical) world that God made. While some might see the material realm as kind of shabby and secondary compared to spiritual or intellectual realities, the Bible does not take this view. Not at all. In the Scriptures, the physical world is very good. It is meant to be the receptacle (or better yet, a temple) that would contain the very presence of God.[3] And as we will later see, the physical realm is so far from being inherently evil that God can even take up flesh within it in the person of Jesus Christ without becoming "gross" or "sinful." Yes, things have been broken now by sin, but this underlying goodness is important to remember when it comes time to think about the sacredness of things like our physical bodies, God's gift of human sexuality, and the way we ought to steward the material world that God has given us. Even in the book of Job, the singing stars and shouting angels speak to the inherent goodness of God's creation.

But what good is this to Job? After all, the reality for him was that he had lost everything! Who cares if God told a thundering story about the way the world began?! It's a fair point. But before heading too far down this path, perhaps we should notice Job's response. The Bible says that after hearing from God, *Job worshipped*. Right there in the middle of the loss and the hurt and the million questions left unanswered, Job worshipped his Creator. Why?

Perhaps it has something to do with the fact that glimpsing the way the story *starts* gives us hope for the way it will *end*. Despite appearances to the contrary, God is on the throne, and this world did not come into being by a random explosion of cosmic gas or cosmic rage. We need to hear that sometimes. Things may be difficult now. Things may be terrible. But the story didn't start that way. And the message of the Creator is that it won't end that way either: not for Job, and not for us.

Logos

So creation started with a party. It began with an eruption of purposeful joy. But what else should we know?

In the New Testament, the Gospel of John fills in another detail for us. Apparently stars and angels were not the first to join the party. They were fashionably late. Because not even they were there in the (very) beginning. John says it this way:

> In the beginning was the [*logos*], and the [*logos*] was with God, and the [*logos*] was God . . . Through him [that is, the *logos*] all things were made. (John 1:1–3)

Which is nice, I guess. But *what* is a *logos*?

Just a few lines further in John's book we learn the strange and intriguing truth toward which the entire Bible points with wonder. This *logos*, or "Word" (as it's translated), comes to us as a first-century Jew named Jesus. The Word is a man, is God, is Jesus. If this seems confusing to you, then you can join twenty centuries of Christians trying to wrap their minds around a person who defies *all* our categories.

Creation from community, John tells us, is not just about stars and angels cheering (metaphorically or otherwise) from the balcony. It's not about created spectators to divine pyrotechnics. It goes much deeper. Creation from community, John tells us, is about a God with room within himself for perfect communion. Jesus (the *logos*) was *with* God; he was *in* God, and he actually *was God* from the eternal beginning. Everything was made through him.

Say goodbye, John says, to your images of a lonely old man with a beard. Say goodbye to a Morgan Freeman deity. This God not only *likes* community, this God *is* community.[4] But it gets better.

From John to Genesis

A quick turn from John to Genesis shows another figure—a third figure—who shares in the eternal life of God in the beginning. The first paragraph of the Bible hints at this. It says that in the beginning: "the Spirit of God was hovering over the waters" (Gen. 1:2).

At this point, the earth is depicted as chaotic and empty. Yet there is something—no, someone—hovering just above the fray. This someone is the Spirit of God, and the Spirit has a part in creation also.

In the Hebrew language (and the Greek for that matter) the word for Spirit is the same as that for breath—Spirit. Creation, then, is what happens when *Breath* gives voice to *Word*. It's a metaphor. Yet it points to truth. The Spirit hovers, waiting. The Word is with God, waiting. And then it happens. A voice says: "Let there be light," and there is (Gen. 1:30). Creation happens when God *speaks*. This metaphor is fascinating, in part, because when we speak, at least a couple things are necessary. We must have breath. And we must form words. It's a cooperative effort that flows forth from a single being. This is how the Bible views creation: God *speaks* the world into existence with wind and words, language and lungfuls, *Spirit* and *Logos*.

God is one. Yet there is relationship within him too: creation *from* community. Instead of a lonely old man, we see a united, three-fold cooperation. And if you had time to reflect upon this three-part harmony—say, for centuries—you might end up referring to it as a kind of triple-unity. A tri-unity. A Trinity.

It is all too much to wrap your mind around, but the main idea is surprisingly simple: creation in the Bible emerges neither from conflict (see Sugar Momma's bloody corpse), nor from a lonely old man in the sky. Creation comes forth from a unified and loving relationship. And this divine communion gives birth to a human one.

Enter Actors

In Genesis 2, God makes a person: Adam. But even in a sin-free world, Adam doesn't do well by himself. Something is missing. So God says this:

> "It is not good for the man to be alone." . . . So the LORD God caused the man to fall into a deep sleep; and while he was sleeping, he took one of the man's ribs and then closed up the place with flesh. Then the LORD God made a woman from the rib he had taken out of the man, and he brought

> her to the man. The man said, "This is now bone
> of my bones and flesh of my flesh; she shall be
> called 'woman,' for she was taken out of man."
>
> That is why a man leaves his father and
> mother and is united to his wife, and they become
> one flesh. Adam and his wife were both naked,
> and they felt no shame. (Gen. 2:18, 21–25)

That last line is my favorite. They were naked, and they felt no shame. Another Christian writer observes that the more you read this passage, the more you begin to understand that "nudity is the point."[5] I think he's right, but we'll come back to that thought in a minute.

Aside from the odd reference to nudity, the first thing that jumps out is that despite the goodness of creation, there is one thing that *isn't* good. To quote the immortal words of *Sesame Street*, "one of these things is *not* like the others . . . one of these things just doesn't belong."

In the midst of this *good* creation, God spots Adam sitting between a baboon and a butternut squash, and he says emphatically: "It is not good for the man to be alone." I have probably heard this verse a hundred times, but for a long time I never fully grasped its meaning.

Lessons from the Hospital

Not long ago, my wife and I were called to the hospital to see some friends that have been especially close to us. This couple, a loving husband and wife, had recently made the long drive to be at our wedding. And in this case, they had driven again to visit their children in college. During this visit, they had gone for a walk. They were holding hands. And as they stepped into a crosswalk, both were slammed by an out-of-control vehicle. She was killed. He broke a leg.

It was gut-wrenching. Soon after, Brianna and I sat with the family in the hospital. During that time, I overheard someone say that in the accident the husband's eye glasses had been flung wildly across the pavement. The next day, someone realized the glasses were missing. So one of the sons went to see if he could find them. Incredibly, he did. The fragile wire frames had been thrown to the side of the road where they sat all day and night with cars and trucks and bicycles rumbling past them. Amazingly, they were still in decent shape. A little bent, but not unwearable.

A while later, I remember someone talking about the glasses and commenting about how *fortunate* the husband was to get them back. Somehow, the discovery struck me differently. I fumed at God with Job-like questions: Why, in all his grand omnipotence, had God seen fit to preserve a pair of glasses, while letting a precious woman die just feet away? It seemed random and stupid. It still does. Not all stories end with greeting card clichés.

We left the hospital soon after. But just before the husband went to surgery, I watched as another friend bent down close to speak with him. "Can you tell me what you're most afraid of?" he asked. The response was brief but penetrating: "being alone."

It is not good for man to be alone.

At the beginning of the Bible, God looks upon loneliness and gives his unvarnished opinion: it is *contra Deum* (against God, and against his will). To the go-at-it-alone existence that we sometimes admire in America, God shouts words of exorcism: "Get out! You do not belong!" As human beings, we were not only created *from* community (Father, Son, and Spirit), we were created *for* community. We were created to do life together—with God and with each other—so Adam gets a soul mate. And she's naked too.

Naked without Shame

Back in junior high I used to have strange nightmares. In some of these, I would show up to school, and about halfway through geometry, a strange question would begin to formulate: *I wonder if I'm wearing pants?*

And, of course, in my dream, I was not. So for the rest of the class I tried to conceal the fact that I was naked. Normally this would seem ridiculous, but in my dreams things like that don't seem to occur to me. In my dream-logic, I think that if I can position my textbook just right *maybe* no one will notice. But they always do. Dreams are cruel that way.

That's the thing about nakedness: it often comes with a side of shame. It's why interrogators have been known to strip their prisoners. It's why robbing someone of their clothes is a way of robbing them of their dignity. But apparently it did not start that way. Genesis says that the man and the woman were naked, yet they felt no shame. By way of definition, it is sometimes said that we feel guilt for things we've *done*, yet we feel shame for who we *are* at some deep level. While guilt may have positive aspects (like driving us toward repentance and change), shame is more insidious. Shame is destructive because it can destroy the very engine and ability to make changes.[6] In the beginning, humans had no word for shame, and thus, no word for clothes. Which is strange, but also rather nice.

The reason has something to do with the way deep communion was always meant to function. We were meant to experience relationships with God, people, and our world without pretense, without makeup, and without shame. That's what "naked community" (now speaking metaphorically) is all about.

If we have a hard time imagining this kind of community, it is probably because we have grown up in a world where getting naked (both literally and metaphorically) is always risky. I'll say that again. It is *always* risky. There is always a chance that someone will point and laugh, take advantage, or be unfaithful. In our fallen context, there is always a chance that someone will judge, exploit, betray, belittle, or just grow bored when they see us for who we really are. In our world, being naked carries risks—as some of you will know quite painfully. Thus the nightmares.

Naked Communion

What we see in Scripture—in books like Job, John, and Genesis—is that when God's Story began, things were different. At the end of the beginning, the image we have is that of two people, standing naked, completely open, completely known, and yet completely unashamed. This is about far more than just a lack of clothing. It is about a kind of living that allows others to see us for who we are, without judgment or fear.

A writer named Paul speaks in the New Testament of how this existence has been fractured. In poetic terms, Paul comes back to the theme of naked unhidden community. As of now, he says, we *know* God and other people only in part. As of now, there are parts of us we hide. There are parts we fake. And there are parts we don't even understand ourselves. We hurt those we care about. We lower our gaze to avoid the eyes of a stranger. Our loves are real but fractured, and we feel it in our bones. Things are not as they ought to be. We *know* in part.

Why is this?

Why are even beautiful things now broken? That is a subject for chapter 2. For now, though, Paul wants to reassure us that a day is coming when creation-style community will make a roaring comeback. This fractured world will be restored. And the result of this will be a kind of naked, unashamed knowing that we can only dream about. We will know in full, even as we are fully known (see 1 Corinthians 13:12). Community will rally.

As Christians we believe this, in part, because our story does not begin with conflict. Conflict may lie at the heart of other theories on creation. It may be the reason why Sugar Momma had to die. But our story is different. Our plotline emerges *from* and *for* loving relationships. We come *from* and *for* communion.

Engage the Story

Having read about the creation chapter in God's Story, it's time now to engage with it yourself. Read the following passages this week, reflect upon their meaning, and be prepared to discuss them with others. Keep in mind that each passage sheds light upon God's character as the Creator in different ways.

- Genesis 1–2
- Psalm 8
- John 1:1–14
- Acts 17:24–28
- Colossians 1:15–20

Discuss the Story

1. In this chapter, we saw that the biblical origins story is unique among other ancient (and modern) options because it centers *not* on creation from conflict, but rather creation from and for community. Reread the following statement from the chapter and discuss the questions below.

   What we discover, when we read the Scriptures carefully, is that the universe emerges not from violent or sexual conflict, not from the clash of volatile personalities or volatile cosmic gases, but *from* and *for* community.

   - Have you ever thought about the biblical origins story as being unique in this way?

- What are some implications of having a view of the world that originates in loving community rather than violent conflict?

2. Use the following statement to discuss the questions below:

   The story of creation is not the tale of a lonely deity looking for companionship. God wasn't reading the personal ads when he crafted the galaxies. The Creator did not make the universe because he needed some interesting people to hang out with.

   - Do you think that it is still common for people to picture God as a solitary old man in the sky?
   - What is wrong with this perspective and how does this explanation of the Trinity change the discussion?

3. When Job's life was falling apart, God didn't give him an answer to the problem of pain, but a picture of creation. Read the following statement and discuss the questions below:

   In a moment of anger and suffering, God grasps Job by the collar and gives him the only thing that will quiet him long enough to trust him through the pain. It's not a greeting card cliché or a Sunday school answer. It is a ringside seat to the bowel-shaking formation of the heavens and the earth.

   - At what point in your own life have you felt a bit like Job? Have you ever experienced a deep loss of community and hope?

- Why do you think God answered Job's complaint in this way?

4. Read Genesis 2:18–25 together and respond to the statement below:

From the very beginning, God looks on loneliness and gives his honest opinion: it is not good. To the go-it-alone existence that we sometimes admire in America, God all but shouts: You don't belong here! Not here! Not now! Not good! And he says this, I think, because as human beings we were not only created *from* community (Father, Son, and Holy Spirit), we were created *for* community. We were created to do life together.

- Do you think our culture looks highly upon individuals who *go it alone*?
- Recall the story of the man who lost his wife. Comment on a time in your own life when it sunk in for you that it is *not good* to be alone.
- Take a moment to consider the people whom God has brought into your life to enrich it. What have these communal relationships meant to you?

5. Read the statement below and then discuss the questions that follow:

At the end of the creation chapter in God's Story, the image we are left with is that of two people, standing naked, completely open, completely known, and yet completely unashamed. However you interpret this, one thing is certain: it is about much more than just a lack of clothing. It is about a kind of living that allows others to see us for who we are, without judgment, ridicule, or fear.

- Without snickering, comment on the importance of the phrase you just read in Genesis: "they were naked without shame."
- Why is this phrase a metaphorical description of true community?

6. Having read the first chapter in God's plotline (creation *from* and *for* community), reflect on these issues in your own life over the next week:

- Am I living in meaningful community right now?
- Are there people in my life who know me well enough to ask me how I'm doing, and really mean it?
- Am I connected to a Jesus community (a.k.a. "a church") in ways that reveal my true belief that our story begins with persons in loving relationships?
- What is the one thing that I can do this week to pursue a life of community both with the Creator, and with other people?

THE FALL

Why Apples Are like A-Bombs

Ever since I was a child I've had a certain fear of snakes. There's just something about them. Some animals are cute—and some are not. Snakes are *not*. Not everyone feels this way, of course. For those of a certain age, you may recall a guy with the Van Halen hair, a Black Sabbath T-shirt, and a terrarium that he kept in the basement. He loves snakes. Just ask him. And then there's the other guy, from the county fair, who never misses an opportunity to parade around with Lulu the pet python coiled around him like a fashion accessory.

But those people are exceptions. The rest of us are made a little nervous by the creatures. Maybe it's the slithering, or the forked tongue, or the portrayals in movies and on TV. Then again, maybe it's the thought of a legless lizard latching onto your jugular, injecting battery acid, and causing you to flail about like a manic celebrity on *Dancing with the Stars*. Yeah, maybe that's it.

When I was little, our family went to visit a distant relative who still lived on the family farm. It was supposed to be an educational experience. It was a chance for the kids to visit the homestead, hear some stories, and perhaps contract a tick-borne illness. Stuff like that. So for the better part of a day we walked around the farm, between tumbleweeds and rusted tractors, as someone showed us where the old house was and where the cast from *Little House on the Prairie* used to fend off wolves and churn the butter. It was a good day. Then somewhere in the middle of the tour, we paused for a few moments by a dilapidated barn. You know what's coming.

As we stood there in the entrance of the creaking structure, I remember my little sister beginning to swing herself around a wooden pole that ran from the dirt floor to the dusty rafters. While the adults were talking, she wrapped her little fingers around the pole and spun around in that way that makes people over the age of eighteen sick to their stomachs.

I'm not sure how long she did this. But eventually someone took the time to notice the small depression that lay at the base of the pole. Coiled snugly inside was an enormous rattlesnake—who was just now beginning to shake his backside faster than Beyoncé at the Super Bowl halftime show.

Someone screamed! People scrambled. And somewhere in the midst of the chaos, a parent grabbed my sister and pulled her away to safety. No one died.

(Except the snake.) No one was even bitten. Yet somewhere in the midst of the commotion, perhaps while I was running like a politician from the truth, I grasped another reason for my distaste of all things serpentine. It's not *just* that we've been virtually preprogramed to dislike the creatures. And it's not *just* that a few of them happen to be dangerous. That's part of it, of course, but there's more.

For me, another thing about snakes, and a further reason why I fear them more than some more dangerous animals (e.g., rabid possums, blood-thirsty ice weasels), is the fact that snakes *surprise* us. Think about that for a moment. For obvious reasons, snakes sneak up on us in ways that cows and donkeys and golden retrievers do not. We don't see them coming. They slither up beneath the shrubbery. They startle us, *even* when they've been there all along.

Surprised by a Serpent

It happens in the Bible too. In Genesis, the surprise comes *one sentence* after some of the happiest words ever uttered: "naked and unashamed." Life is fresh and good. It's the honeymoon after the wedding night of Genesis 2. Then right in the middle of Sandals Mesopotamia, we're surprised by a serpent. And if that weren't enough, he (the snake) starts asking questions. "Did God really say, 'You must not eat from any tree in the garden'?" (Gen. 3:1). It's a loaded query, especially coming from an animal—and the whole scene leaves us scratching our heads. It raises questions:

Question: Where did this crafty serpent come from?
Answer: God made him.
Question: *Why*?
Answer: . . .

The writer of Genesis doesn't tell us much about the snake. The story just moves on. Hence, we're left wondering: Why would a loving Creator allow a crafty talking serpent into a world where he could mislead the happy honeymooners? Why would God do this? No answer. But the snake does teach us something crucial about God's Story. It's a lesson we'd do well to learn early in our study of the Bible. Here it is: *the universe is complicated*. Not every question that we have is answered by the Scriptures.

Despite what some Christians would like to believe, God's Story is more beautiful and complex than an after-school special or a 1970s sitcom. In the Bible, there are surprises, unanswered questions, and not every episode ends with the cast all smiling, freeze-framed into the camera. *There's a snake in the garden*. And from the moment we look down and see him coiled there on the page, that previously mentioned lesson hits us: the universe is complicated.

To many of us, this is hardly welcome news. Complexity is frustrating. If you're like me, you like things simple. Most of us do. We like things cut-and-dried. We like bullet points and bottom lines. But as we dive into God's Story we discover that the Bible disavows such false simplicity. There are some answers we'll have to wait to hear. And while we may be uncomfortable with that, the Bible doesn't seem to be. It's as if the writer embraces a complex reality without feeling the need to extrapolate. "Oh yeah, did I mention there is a crafty talking snake? Now on with the story."

Having noticed such unresolved complexities, we can choose to see them in one of two ways. Option One: we can view them as *proof* that the Bible is a ridiculous fiction that should be discarded. Many intelligent people have chosen this path, and it is a realistic option. "Snakes don't talk!" we shout. "And anyway, where's he fit within God's *good* creation?" To the first point (the talking animals one), we should say that ancient people were well aware of this reality. They didn't see the world as one big Disney film in which all the creatures sang and spoke life lessons to wayward princesses. And as to the next question about where the serpent fits amid the goodness of God's world, we might note the following: the Bible never states that the creation was safe; it only says that it was "very good." And while this goodness seems to rule out the presence of human sin in the beginning, it apparently does not rule out the presence of a tempter in the garden.

If Option One is to cry foul at the first sign of unexplained anomalies within the Bible, Option Two is to remain open in the face of the unanswered questions. We are dealing, after all, with the subject of an infinite and transcendent God. What's more, this God reveals himself through literature written (in some cases) millennia ago and filtered through the personalities of ancient people who do not share our language or our customs. Perhaps, then, we should not expect everything to make perfect sense according to the criteria of modern thought. If it did, we could be quite sure that we invented it.

Having said all that, if we sit within this strange story long enough, we may begin to see that even the oddities often bear the tell-tale marks of life as it is—that is, complex, and (gratefully) lacking in simplistic Sunday school answers. Because as any scientist can tell you: *real things* are complicated. C. S. Lewis made this point by referring to an item as common as a kitchen table. When you look at it from a distance, Lewis said, it seems quite boring—perhaps just wood and nails and finish:

> But ask a scientist to tell you what it is really made of—all about the atoms and how the light waves rebound from them and hit my eye and what they do to the optic nerve and what it does to my brain—and, of course, you find that what we call "seeing a table" lands you in mysteries and complication which you can hardly get to the end of.[1]

Translation: real things are not simple. Reality is mysterious and complicated.

Some of us have caught a glimpse of this truth while lying on a bed of grass and inspecting the world of creepy-crawly things that move unseen beneath our feet. We glimpse this tiny world living in our lawn, and we know our ecosystem is complex. The world is mysterious. So am I. And because of this, I need to inhabit a story that is at least as complex as I am. To be clear, this open perspective remains a far cry from somehow proving that all of Scripture's claims are true. Jesus never promised to answer all our questions. And the quest for certainty can be an idol. Still, for those of us who sense the underlying mystery in our world, even some of the question marks within the Bible can begin to have the ring of truth. There is a snake in God's good garden. It's complicated.

Why Freud Was Right

To review, chapter 2 in the biblical storyline (the one we sometimes call "the fall") opens with a talking serpent. But as Sigmund Freud would likely tell us, sometimes a snake is *more* than just a snake. As we read on, we begin to see that the crafty talking serpent represents something—or someone—far darker than just a scaly legless lizard. There is a villain in this story. There is an enemy, an accuser. And while Genesis says little of this dark spiritual force, the book of Revelation gives us some other names for Eden's hissing tempter. He is "that ancient serpent called the devil, or Satan, who leads the whole world astray" (Rev. 12:9). So while creation is born without human sin, it doesn't stay that way.

If chapter 1 is about creation *from* and *for* community, chapter 2 is about the way things fall apart. But more importantly, the story of the fall is not just about something that happened way back then. It's about something that happens now. It's not just about the fall, it's also about *falling*. It's *our story*, not just that of Adam and Eve. It's for everyone who has watched as their life and dreams and plans come apart at the seams. It's about broken marriages, broken hearts, death, and dead-end jobs. It's about falling, and all of us do that.

Chapter 2 in God's long Story starts with a talking snake, but it gets going when we talk back. A conversation takes place between the serpent and a person. God's truth and goodness are questioned (that's how sin almost always starts), and then it happens. The honeymooners thumb their noses at the Creator, and things are never the same (see Genesis 3:2–7). Creation starts with naked, honest community. But it's by the tree that we begin to sense that even naked and honest community is vulnerable. To quote the poet John Milton, things are "happy, but for so happy, ill secur'd."[2] In the story, they want to be like God but in the wrong kind of way (see Genesis 3:5). Normally, we would think that being God-like is a virtue. But it isn't always. There is a vast difference between mirroring God's faithfulness and parroting his power. Sometimes a desire to be like God is actually a desire to *be* god—or rather, to be my own god. And when that happens, suddenly just being my naked self isn't what it used to be.

We could spend hours dissecting this chapter. Almost every word in Genesis 3 is an exit ramp along the highway of biblical understanding. And many exits lead to interesting places. Unfortunately, there isn't time for much sightseeing. We need to see the big picture of the fall, and we need to answer just a few of the big questions that emerge after reading this part of the story. Questions like: How does a simple bite of fruit result in a fatal fracture of the whole creation? How does that happen?!

Apples and A-Bombs

It's a simple question really. How does a seemingly insignificant choice have such cataclysmic consequences? Some of us who have read the story a hundred times have become immune to this strangeness, but that's not necessarily a good thing. The strangeness *ought* to strike us.

In the beginning, God builds a lovely biosphere. He places people in it, he puts them in charge, then he tells them to eat at any restaurant they wish—except for *this* one. This one is off-limits. This eatery is taboo. In fact, if the happy honeymooners should visit this forbidden restaurant—the one just up the street, with the delicious entrees and the snooty waiters—they will trigger a chain reaction more terrible than a nuclear bomb.

It's a peculiar story, and it raises questions. Why is this God such a controlling kill-joy? I mean, really! What's the big deal with a piece of fruit? Isn't this just one more example of pointless religious legalism? "Eat from this tree, and I'll kill you!"

These questions may be honest ones, but I'd like to suggest that they are not the best ones. Because just as Christians sometimes get caught up on squabbles over talking snakes, so too can we miss the forest of Genesis 3 for our talk of fruit and trees. As with Genesis 1–2, we cannot read this story with the same wooden literalism as we would a copy of *USA Today*. Especially if it was never intended to be read like that. Don't just ask why the serpent talks; pay attention to what he *says*.[3] In its ancient way, Genesis 3 gives what Christians believe to be a true and moving picture of how sin wormed its way into our world.

Perhaps the command against eating from a particular tree may have less to do with an apple (which is never mentioned), and more to do with a missed *opportunity* to fulfill the human calling. Here's what I mean.

When God blesses Adam and Eve with the status of his image-bearers, this blessing brings a calling. They are to "image" (or reflect God's will) within God's world. And in so doing, they are to *rule* and *care for* God's creation in ways that honor him. One translation says that humans were placed in the garden "to work it and take care of it" (Gen. 2:15)—which means (among other things) that conservation matters to the God of the Bible. We are commanded to steward the good world that God has given us, both then and now.

More specifically, the image-bearers are to: "rule over the fish in the sea and the birds in the sky, over the livestock and all the wild animals, and over all the creatures that move along the ground" (Gen. 1:26). To be clear, that last part includes the snakes—regardless of their verbal skills. But what does it mean to rule over animals? The language could conjure up odd images of a kingly figure perched on a tree stump, surrounded by a royal court of squirrels, rabbits, and field mice. So why does God give Adam and Eve this peculiar vocation? And come to think of it, why does he reiterate the same command, just a few verses later: "God blessed them [Adam and Eve] and said to them, . . . 'Rule over the fish in the sea and the birds in the sky and over every living creature that moves on the ground'" (Gen. 1:28).

I'd like to suggest a simple possibility. Perhaps the reason God reiterates the command to rule over the animals is *not* that he wants Adam to set up a literal serfdom with chimps for knights, and monkeys for court jesters.

Perhaps one reason for the command's repetition is that God is preparing Adam and Eve for a *showdown* with an animal that moves across the garden floor.[4] To be more specific, God is preparing the honeymooners for a showdown with a snake that, as Freud would tell us, is more than just a snake.

The setting for this showdown is a tree. And this matters too. In the Ancient Near East, prominent trees often served as both the courtrooms and the gallows of the day. If a king's commands had been spit upon, the offenders would be taken to a large tree and judged under its branches. If found guilty they would then be strung up, quite literally, as a sign that justice had been done. This was the world inhabited by the first readers of Genesis. It was the world they understood. Thus the ancients may have known exactly what Adam *should* have done to anyone denying the commands of the King.[5]

The showdown at the tree was not just a sneak attack by a crafty serpent. Nor was it a pointless bit of religious legalism. No, the showdown at the tree was an *opportunity*. It was an opportunity for Adam and Eve to do what rulers always did to traitors under trees.

In commanding Adam and Eve to rule over the animals, God was granting the honeymooners both the *authority* and the *opportunity* to crush the head of evil before it could grow and worm its way into everything.

It was an opportunity to make the universe a safer place for generations to come. It was a chance to make sure words like "rape," "hunger," and "Reality TV" never entered the human vocabulary. (You heard me.)

This is what the conversation at the tree is about. It is an opportunity for Adam and Eve to exercise their divine authority and do at the beginning of the story what God must later do at the end. The conversation at the tree is an opportunity for humans to put evil in its place and secure a future in which true community would flourish. As we will see, this dream is not lost forever, but it will take a far more terrible tree to resurrect it from the ashes.

This is the point so often missed when Christians talk about the fall. The tragedy of the honeymooners was not so much about an apple that was eaten. The tragedy was about an *opportunity* that was missed. God's command was not given simply to fulfill some bit of religious legalism. It was given to make the world a better place. And this insight about the first sin tells us something about all the ones that follow.

The Thing about Sin

I met a young woman long ago who was having questions about her faith. These were real questions, mind you, not the superficial style-of-the-music variety that pastors sometimes have to spend their time on. These were genuine questions. She told me her primary problem with Jesus and the Bible and the whole faith-thing was not that she didn't believe in a God, but that she didn't understand why certain things were considered, well, *sinful*.

"Don't take this the wrong way," she told me, "but I just don't get it!" She was looking a little embarrassed. "I mean, I'm not married," she said, "and I don't know if I ever will be. But I don't understand why God should care if someone like me were to go out and have sex. Why is it any of God's business? Why is *that* a *sin*?! How do I know it's not just a random rule made up by some fundamentalist prude?"

It is a fair question. And it boils down to an even shorter one: Why is sin, *sin*? In other words, why does sin bother God? And why should it bother us?

Importantly, this is precisely the kind of question that can't be answered by those who see the Bible merely as a cosmic rulebook. Rules are great at telling us *what*. They can tell you not to spit on the sidewalk, sleep with your girlfriend, or pull the little tag off the bottom of your sofa. Rules are great at telling you *what*. But rules are terrible at telling you *why*.

And this is one reason why the Bible-as-mere-rulebook approach makes things so frustrating for people who have honest questions. It's why it can be frustrating when well-meaning Christians answer every question with: "Because the Bible says so." In its most exaggerated form, the conversation sometimes goes like this:

Question: Why shouldn't I do X?
Answer: Because God says so.
Question: Why?
Answer: Because if you do X, you might burn in hell.

And this is where things usually end. There's something about the threat of eternal damnation that has a way of throwing a wet blanket on a conversation. So why is sin, sin? What would you say?

The Fullest Kind of Existence

As I listened to this woman, I couldn't help but think about the story of Adam and Eve. I thought about how God wanted the best for them. God wanted them to live a life of harmony with creation, peace with their Creator, peace within themselves, and love between each other. Jesus called this kind of existence: life to the full (see John 10:10).

This is why (in the story) God gave them so many good things: good food, good sex, good stuff as far as they could see. God wanted us to have the best kind of life. Perhaps this is also why God gave humans the opportunity to judge evil at the tree, instead of crafting us entirely as a race of robots. Love requires some amount of freedom. So God gave people the opportunity to be his *stewards* of creation, and to strike the deathblow against evil. It was a profound opportunity. But in the story, Adam and Eve choose to reject the good life for a cheap generic knockoff. They reject lasting fulfillment for a momentary craving, and it hurt them the same way it hurts us.

Rather than enjoy peace with the Creator, Adam and Eve hide from God. Rather than enjoy confidence within themselves, they feel uncomfortable in their own skin. They reach for fig leaves because they feel ashamed.

Rather than enjoy love between each other, they begin to pass the buck. They blame each other and they blame God. Rather than enjoy harmony with their environment, they now fight against the soil in order to enjoy its fruit. To quote W. B. Yeats, "things fall apart." And we all can attest to that reality.

Not all of this went through my mind before I answered the young woman's question. But enough of it did that I decided to respond with something different than: "Because the Bible says so." I told her that I thought God wanted us to live the very best kind of life—not an easy life, mind you, but the best kind of life. Jesus called it "life to the full." And because I believe this, I also believe that sin is not just an arbitrary breaking of a religious rule (like pulling the tag off the underside of a sofa). It is an offense against God's perfect holiness. And it is also a destructive jab against the *shalom* (peace) that God wants for our world. But in addition to these traditional answers, sin is also something else. Get this. *Sin is a choice to embrace an inferior existence.* It's like drinking dirty water from polluted wells.[6] It may not seem like it at the time, but it is—in every single instance. It's like choosing a TV dinner over filet mignon. And because of this, when viewed rightly, God's commands are actually conduits to deeper joy (more on this in later chapters).[7]

Of course, there are religious rules that God wants nothing to do with. There are extra add-on rules that have more in common with the sofa tag than the God of the Bible. There are legalists today, just as there were in Jesus' time. And they need confronting. Yet as I read the story of creation, I am more convinced that obeying the

God seen in the Scriptures truly is the best way to live. I am more and more convinced that treating others like people instead of products is a more gratifying existence. Sacrifice is more fulfilling than selfishness, conservation is more satisfying than reckless consumption, and sexual fidelity is more satiating than a fleeting Vegas escapade.

I said this to the woman (though in fewer words) and then I asked her something else. I asked her if at some level she already sensed as much. Because at some level, all of us have a sense that what the crafty talking serpents have been telling us isn't quite working. For most of us, just like Adam and Eve, it doesn't take a booming voice from above to tell us that our choices haven't ended up the way we hoped. I find it interesting that the first humans hid themselves before God ever came searching for them. We do the same. We have our own fig leaves. We hide behind long work days, full schedules, and the drone of a television. We hide too.

We fill our days with activity and our nights with distraction. And we do it because we know as well as the first humans that our choices have damaged us. We know it; and we don't need a preacher, or a prophet, or a shrink to tell us. You believe in the fall because you've experienced it. It's not just a part of the biblical story; it's a part of yours too. And it hurts.

Even so, the British writer G. K. Chesterton reminds us that this painful portion of the story actually contains some good news hidden deep within it. He wrote, "The Fall is . . . the only encouraging view of Life. It holds . . . that we have misused a good world, and not merely been entrapped into a bad one."[8] Rather than evil having been baked into our world from the beginning or, worse, baked into God, such evil is actually an intruder.

And that is not the only good news to be found in Genesis 3. In spite of humans raising their fists to God's loving rule, there is mercy to be found within this text. While the serpent and the ground are cursed, the humans are not cursed (despite what you may have heard). They face consequences to be sure, but God never curses them. Go back and read it for yourself. Instead, God *clothes* his sinful people (see Genesis 3:21). And these garments have at least two meanings. First, they cover our shame—which is something God wants to do for you as well. And second, they symbolize that they have been made God's heirs (his inheritors) once more. This is the symbolism that is present all throughout the Bible with the giving of a sacred garment to one's child. God clothes Adam and Eve just as the father in Jesus' famous parable does his prodigal son (see Luke 15:22). The clothes mean that you are still his beloved child. And while you may be ashamed of you, he is not.

But even that is not the end of the hope that comes seeping through in this dark chapter. In Genesis 3:15 we receive a promise that is sometimes called "the first gospel." We are told that, one day, the "seed" (son) of the woman will crush the serpent's head, even as the serpent strikes his heel. In this cryptic prophecy, some see a kind of double deathblow. The snake will die and so too the Son. Whatever could this mean? How could such a death bring victory?

After Eden: Genesis 3–11

Genesis 3–11 show how a missed opportunity spirals into a cycle of pain and violence. There are moments of joy. But even these are bittersweet. Adam and Eve give birth to sons and sibling rivalries. Their children multiply, but as they do, their memories of the garden fade. There are accomplishments. There is progress. People learn and grow. They raise livestock, build tools, instruments, and even cities. But despite their numbers and proximity, they often lack communion. Like some of us, they live together but alone. The cycle of selfishness crescendos.

It gets so bad at one point that God decides to start all over. In one of the most shockingly toned-down Sunday school stories of all time, the Creator judges the creation through the blunt instrument of a colossal flood. Yet even this judgment does not solve the problem. It is as if the tale of the flood is meant, in part, to demonstrate that even the best among us carry the fatal virus. Noah ends up drunk and naked in his tent—proving once again that misusing God's good fruit (this time of the vine) has painful consequences. The pathogen is now a part of us, despite our corresponding potential (by God's grace) for acts of beauty, brilliance, and compassion. This is what it means to be fallen. It is to have the dual status of having been made *from* and *for* communion, while also being pulled backward toward sin and shame and death. Apart from God, not one of us resists the pull.[9]

So humanity begins to fill the earth again, and once more the good God gets forgotten. They build a city and a tower with a high-tech wonder called "the brick"—not much bigger than a smartphone (remember that point).

Unfortunately, the building program, like many others, is merely a prideful effort "to make a name for ourselves" (Gen. 11:4). And, unfortunately, the high-tech wonder that was supposed to connect everyone across the world leaves us feeling more scattered and divided than ever. Thankfully, we all learned our lesson, though, and that never happened again with new technology.

With the collapse of this tower, called Babel, one begins to wonder if God won't just call it quits. We wonder if he won't just throw up his hands and say to hell with this whole project (literally), to hell with these humans and the way they hurt each other! But he doesn't. And the next chapter proves it. Because amid the dust of a fallen tower in a fallen world, a rescue operation is about to begin, and the story is just getting started.

Apples and Opportunities

Before skipping ahead, however, it is important to remember what the story of the fall has to do with us. In one sense, the talk of an enchanted garden, forbidden fruit, and a talking snake sounds about as real as Snow White and her dwarves. It sounds like a fantasy. Yet in another sense, it strikes us as the most familiar thing imaginable. The fall is as familiar as our own life story because as we look back on the pages of our lives, we can't help but remember our own apples and missed opportunities.

The relationship that went sour, the words we wish we never said, the divorce, that night that still haunts us. We can doubt the existence of the garden, the talking serpent, and the forbidden fruit. But at some level we feel it to be true. As Paul the apostle once put it: all of us have sinned. We've all *fallen* (see Romans 3:23). It's universal. Just turn on the news.

The fall is not just a chapter in God's Story, it's a chapter in ours as well. But there is good news. Things don't end here. Because in the Scriptures snakes may talk, but not even talking serpents get the final say.

Engage the Story

Having read about the fall in God's Story, it's time now to engage with it yourself. Read the following passages this week, reflect upon their meaning, and be prepared to discuss them with others:

- Genesis 3–4
- Genesis 11:1–9
- Romans 5:12–21

Discuss the Story

1. Chapter 2 in God's Story (the one we call the fall) starts with a talking snake, but it really gets going when humanity talks back.

    - Read the conversation between Eve and the serpent in Genesis 3:1–7. Discuss what stands out to you about the way the conversation proceeds.
    - Do you see any connection between this first temptation and the temptations in your own life?

Take some time and look at the progression of emotions and desires within the text.

- Over the last few days or weeks, how were you tempted and what was the result?

2. People sometimes scoff at Christianity for the idea that the results of this first sin could be so cataclysmic. With this criticism in mind, discuss the following questions:

- Has the story of the fall ever seemed strange or ridiculous to you? How so?
- Have you ever seen the command about the forbidden fruit as a pointless bit of religious legalism? Why or why not?
- In what way does God's command (about ruling over the animals and rejecting the forbidden fruit) actually create an occasion for people to judge evil at the beginning of the story? In other words, how was the proverbial apple really an opportunity?

3. Recall the woman who asked the questions, "Why does sin bother God?" In other words, why does God care if we do certain things, and why does God say that some things are off limits?

- How would you answer this young woman's question?
- What about when Jesus says he wants us to live "life to the full"?

4. Read the following statement and discuss the questions below:

For most of us, just like Adam and Eve, it doesn't take a booming voice from above to tell us that our choices haven't ended up the way we hoped. The first humans hid themselves before God ever came searching for them. We do the same. We hide behind fig leaves and long work days, behind the constant drone of a television, or the glow of a smartphone. We fill our days with activity and our nights with distraction. Sometimes, we do it because we know as well as the first humans that our choices have damaged the relationships that matter most—and we don't need a preacher, or a prophet, or a shrink to tell us that.

We believe in the fall because we've experienced it. It's not just a part of God's Story; it's a part of our story too.

- Does this statement ring true to you? How so?
- When in your own life have you made a choice that made you want to hide from God as Adam and Eve did? If the story is appropriate for group discussion, discuss what this experience was like, and what it taught you.
- On the flip side, in what ways have you experienced the effects of the fall apart from a poor choice that you made yourself? In other words, how does sin hurt us even when we are not the ones at fault?

5. Read Romans 3:23–24 aloud together from your Bibles.

In this passage, Paul talks about the way in which we are all sinful. We have all fallen short of God's will for our lives. Yet there is hope. Paul also references the way in which God has begun to reverse the curse through Jesus. In light of the forgiveness offered through Christ, take a moment to reflect on the following questions together, or silently through a time of repentance and/or confession.

- Over the past days and weeks, how have the effects of the fall wormed their way into my own life?
- In what ways have I sensed the brokenness of this world?
- In the past weeks or months, how have I repeated the sin of Adam and Eve by distrusting God and seeking selfish interests over the good of others?
- Knowing that God calls me to true repentance, how can I make amends with people I have hurt, even if it is uncomfortable?

6. Although the fall is a painful chapter in God's plot-line, in the Scriptures snakes may talk, but not even talking serpents get the final say.

- Spend a moment thanking God that his grace gets the final say in our lives. How have you experienced that grace and redemption in spite of sin and brokenness?

ISRAEL

Why Wrestlers Need Rescuing

The LORD said to Abram, "Go from your country, your people and your father's household to the land I will show you.

"I will make you into a great nation,
and I will bless you;
I will make your name great, and you will be a blessing.
. . . all peoples on earth
will be blessed through you." (Gen. 12:1–3)

Suppose that someone were to give you the task of fixing *all* the world's problems. In case you're wondering, that means *everything* from hunger and greed to long lines at the ladies' restroom. Where would you begin? Or better yet, who would you choose to help you?

In the Scriptures, we're surprised to discover that God's plan to save creation starts in the unlikeliest of places. In fact, when God is faced with the task of restoring a fractured world, he looks all the obvious helpers in the eye, and calmly answers: none of the above. None of these will do. When God sets out to save the world, only one individual catches his attention. Not a general, or a king, or a rock star, but a shriveled-up old man named Abram.

God comes to Abram late in life with a peculiar message: "Abram . . . I want *you* to take a trip." And with that, a new chapter in God's Story opens with just two words: "Abram went."[1]

Abram's Road Trip

Without a map or GPS to guide him, Abram sets out with his wife to an unknown destination. The couple leaves their home, their heritage, and all that is familiar. They just *go*. And the only guarantee they have to cling to is a rather peculiar promise. "One day," God said, "the whole world will be blessed because of you."[2] Along the way, God changes their names: his to Abraham, hers to Sarah. And through many twists and turns, Abraham shows faith in God's unlikely promise. In the New Testament, this theme is taken up as he is known as *both* the man of "faith" and the man of "deeds" (see, for example, Romans 4 and James 2). Both titles are fitting because, as we will see, faith expressing itself in obedience has always been God's desire from his people. Always.

The call of Abraham marks the start of God's grand rescue operation known as "Israel." It begins, not with an army or a celebrity or a gifted politician, but with a geriatric tag team—Abraham and Sarah—wandering through the wilderness. This is God's big idea to fix a broken world: two card-carrying members of the AARP, with camels.

In the end, however, the strange choice of Abraham tells us something important about God's Story. It tells us emphatically that the Creator's way of solving problems is fundamentally different than our own. I'll rephrase that point because it's crucial: when God sets out to fix our troubles, he goes through unlikely channels, unlikely people, and unlikely circumstances. Thus, the Creator's way of solving the problem of sin starts not with military might, human ingenuity, or scientific innovation. It starts with an unlikely family, the family of Abraham and Sarah, the family known as Israel. This is the big idea of this chapter. And it's one worth pondering.

All of us come from families of one kind or another. Whether your birth parents stuck around or not, we all have a biological heritage. Some families are large and some are small. Some are what we now call "broken homes." But the truth is that all families are broken in one way or another. We all carry baggage from our roots. And we all carry gifts. Still, the shocking truth of Scripture is this: God's rescue operation begins with a family that is *at least* as screwed up (and yet, as beautiful) as yours. And for some reason, that ought to give us all some hope.

Many Sons?

Growing up, I used to sing a song about God's family. We learned it in Sunday school. My mom played the piano and us kids would jump around and belt out the melody like little rock stars with clip-on ties. I have pictures. The major lyrical emphasis of the song centered around the idea that "the party of the first part" (father Abraham) had many, many sons.

Well, kind of. Come to find out there actually weren't that many sons to start with. Just two. One named *Yitzhak* (Isaac), he was Abraham's favorite. And another named Ishmael (who Abraham fathered by his servant).

There's not time to go into all the drama surrounding the two brothers, but suffice it to say that Yitzhak grew up, got married, and had a son of his own. He named this son Jacob. And that's how one of the greatest songs in the history of Sunday school-dom got its start.

But for all this father-son talk, Jacob was a momma's boy. And he was also a deceiver. At a time in human history when muscles and masculinity were important, Jacob learned to survive *not* with his brawn, but with his brain. He was a plotter, a conniver, and he had clawed and cheated his way through life. He had done it from birth, when he was born snatching (ambitiously) at the heel of his twin brother—and he was good at it.

Jacob's brother Esau was a jock. He was older (barely), and he was stronger too. Esau liked to hunt and grunt and kill. He had hair on his chest, and everywhere else for that matter (picture: Sasquatch in a tunic). Esau was his father's son. He was meat-and-potatoes; he drove a pickup; he listened to country. Jacob liked to cook; he drove a Prius; he listened to indie-rock.

In other words, Jacob and Esau were siblings, but they were very different. Perhaps you can relate.

Labels

Because Esau was older, he was supposed to get his father's inheritance. He was *supposed* to get it. It never happened. In an act of Jacob-like deception (involving some fake body hair and a recipe for Mommy's bestest soup), the younger brother stole his sibling's birthright. In his conniving way, Jacob took his father's blessing, his brother's inheritance, and with that, the chance to be included in the line of men and women through whom God would work to save the world. Let me say it another way: *Jacob lied his way into God's family tree!* He cheated his way in, and as a result, Yahweh (the one true God of all creation) would forever be known as the God of Abraham, of Isaac, and . . . of Jacob.[3]

If we bristle at this, it is probably because we would like to think of God's family as sort of the Moral Majority of the ancient world (that is, if the Moral Majority had actually been moral). We would like to think of them as Boy Scouts who never lied or cheated or slept around: Billy Grahams in bathrobes and Birkenstocks.

Newsflash: they weren't.

Some were more like this, of course. But most were not. Jacob wasn't even close. Even his name bore testimony to this reality. He was *Jacob* (the heel-grasping deceiver). And the reputation was fitting.[4]

In other words, Jacob was a name, but it was also a *label*.

One doesn't need to read the Bible very long to discover that in the ancient world, like today, being labeled was a tough thing to overcome. From a young age, the taglines given to us have a way of cementing into our subconscious and defining who we are. Labels become a part of our identity. Words like slut, jock, freak—*Jacob*.

Anyone who's been through junior high school knows how badly names can hurt. They can wound us. And they can stick. Yet one thing we discover about God's plot-line is that the Creator has a peculiar habit of changing the labels associated with his children. Throughout the Scriptures, Israel's God has a way of changing names. He did this for Jacob. In the pages that follow, we come to know the deceptive heel-grasper by another name, a better name, and a name that will be used to describe God's family for thousands of years. The name is Israel. It means *wrestler*. And Jacob earned the title.

What's in a Name?

It happened by a brook.

On a starry Middle Eastern night, Jacob the deceiver lay awake beside a babbling stream in the wilderness. He was worried. At the moment, he was once more attempting to connive a way to keep his brother Esau from killing him. He wasn't finding one. After years apart, there was to be a meeting between the brothers. The two grandsons of Abraham were about to come face-to-face, and Jacob was at wit's end. He had spent his whole life running—from his home, from Esau, from the truth. Now it was time to stop.

And so it was that something very strange took place. While Jacob lay awake, the writer says "a man wrestled with him till daybreak" (Gen. 32:24). A *man* struggled with Jacob. The sentence sounds straightforward enough. But beneath the surface, it is one of the oddest stories in the Scriptures. It's strange, because as we read on, we come to see that it is not with just any flesh-and-blood *human* that Jacob struggled. Many scholars argue that Jacob was wrestling with God himself.

The scene defies attempts to picture it. Here is God in human form: the Sovereign One, allowing a lying momma's boy named *Jacob* to claw and bite and snarl at him, while hanging on for dear life. And hang on Jacob does.

After a lifetime of leaving and deceiving, the Scriptures say that Jacob "clung to the Man," and would not let him go. Then the mysterious Visitor asks a fascinating question: "What is your name?" This is the very thing he had lied about to steal his way into the blessing.

But this time, the liar's response is short and true.

"I am *Jacob*" (Gen. 32:27, translation mine).

At face value Jacob's answer may not seem that significant. It's just a name. It may as well have been Ross or Bill or Gertrude. But for Jacob it is more than a name. This time it sounds like a confession. "I am Jacob," he says. I am the deceptive heel-grasper. It's like the statement given by the fugitive after the car chase is over and the evidence is staring him in the face. The cuffs are on and the conniver is finally finished lying. "I am Jacob," he says.

The Wrestler

Jacob confesses his identity and again the unexpected happens. Instead of snapping the deceiver's scrawny neck, God does something else. He changes Jacob's name.

"Your name will no longer be Jacob, but Israel because you have wrestled with God and with men and have overcome" (Gen. 32:28). Your name will be Israel, the *wrestler*.

From this day forward, the children of Jacob possess a singular calling. They possess a role in God's Story unlike any other people. From this day forward, they *are* Israel. They are the Wrestlers. They are to be the family that wrestles with the Creator's unique calling upon their lives to be a light to the nations. They have been chosen to be the bringers of God's rescue. The God of the universe has *selected them* from all the people on the planet to be a part of an operation to restore creation. This was the meaning of God's covenant promise made to Abraham: "all peoples on earth will be blessed through you" (Gen. 12:3).

In Christian teaching, God's covenantal choosing is sometimes called "election." But what Israel's calling reveals about God's choice is crucial. Divine election is not primarily about God choosing one person *instead* of the others; rather, it is about God choosing one *for the sake* of the others. The point here is redemptive. The idea is that through God's choice of Israel, all nations, races, tribes, and tongues will have access to salvation. Indeed, even the creation itself will be restored. This is the end-goal of election: God chooses a part for the good of the whole. Again: "all peoples on earth will be blessed through you."[5]

This was the calling with which every son and daughter of Israel would have to struggle. It was the realization to be passed from every Hebrew mother to her child: God chose us, he spoke to us, and he expects something from us. Like Jacob by the brook, the children of *Israel* would wrestle with God's call upon their lives to be a different kind of family, a different kind of community, and a different kind of nation: a holy people. Some would wrestle well. Some would wrestle poorly. But none would escape the struggle.

To Christians today, the call to "grapple" or "struggle" with God's call may seem irreverent or disrespectful. Not so. Apparently, the God of the Bible wants a people who will come to him with their deepest questions, fears, and anxieties. After all, he knows them anyway. One place in which we see this honest wrestling match most vividly is in the poetic literature: books like Psalms and Lamentations. In such places, people like David cry out to God with frightfully uncensored prayers: "My God, my God, why have you forsaken me? Why are you so far from saving me, so far from my cries of anguish?" (see Psalm 22). In spite of such hopeless-sounding cries, however, it often seems that God brings hope to his wrestlers precisely through the act of crying out in honest prayer. Perhaps you can relate.

After Jacob's struggle by the brook, God's family had a name, but they did not have a home. A few hundred years later and not much had changed. Far from being on top of the world, the great-great grandkids of Abraham,

Isaac, and Israel were now *stuck* as slaves in Egypt. And as you may have guessed, there's a story behind that too.

Leaving Boston

Many years ago, I loaded up most of my belongings—including my life-size cardboard cutout of a young Bob Dylan—and I set off on a two-day road trip from Boston, Massachusetts, to the hinterlands of Middle America. I could try to romanticize the trip as a kind of second installment of Jack Kerouac's American odyssey, but mostly it was just two days spent dodging semis, road kill, and text-messaging teenagers who make Britney Spears look like a driver's education instructor.

It was pretty boring. But between intervals of talking to myself and listening to an old Counting Crows box set (I am old), I happened to pop in an old cassette tape (told you) that I found lying inside the console. It was a lecture given by an aging professor of theology.

In a high-pitched, almost cracking voice, the elderly professor was talking about reading the Bible from the perspective of a people who have been systematically enslaved—bought, bred, sold, and exploited—by supposedly Christian oppressors. He was talking about reading the Bible from *below*, from his own perspective as a black man growing up in segregation-era America.[6]

And as he spoke, I could hear his cracking voice grow more and more irate with the questions being posed by the mostly white audience. *They weren't getting it!* he thought. *They weren't asking the right questions!* and it was angering him. He was yelling now and going on about how most of us just couldn't understand where he was coming from.

And I thought maybe he was right. I couldn't understand what it was like to be kicked out of a restaurant because of my skin color. I couldn't understand the implications of being told by a parent *not* to talk to a policeman if ever I should get lost. I couldn't understand because try as I might, as a middle-class white kid growing up in the heartland, I tended to think about slavery and segregation in much the same way that I think about the Great Depression, the great potato famine, or the bubonic plague. "Sure, those were terrible," I'd say, "but didn't they happen a pretty long time ago?" I can't change the past. I can't rewrite history. I'm not a racist. So why did it feel like this old man was yelling at *me* through the tape deck?

Leaving Egypt

I kept these questions in my mind through the state of New York. But the longer cardboard Bob Dylan glowered at me from the backseat—through the mountains of Pennsylvania and the cornfields of Ohio—the more I got to thinking about how God's people had been *slaves* too. They were slaves in Egypt. And the more I thought about it, the more I was convinced that *they* would have understood where this African American professor was coming from. They would have related to him.

Because there is something about slavery that sears itself into your memory. I imagine there is something about it that burns its way into your collective consciousness. It transcends generations. You remember it. It stays with you. And many of us can relate to this only partially.

But we can relate *partially* because, regardless of our backgrounds, we do know what it is like to be treated somewhat like a product. We experience it in subtle ways. The young woman who walks down high school hallways made to feel like fashion runways. The old man who, after a lifetime of independence, is shipped off to die in an ammonia-smelling nursing home. The single mom who, while trying to send her kids to college, finds that her pension has been liquidated by a corporate millionaire who cooked the books. We know what it's like to feel like a *product*, and in a small sense, that's what slavery is about. Slavery is about treating people as products. It's not just about denying rights; it's about denying full humanity.

This is what happened in Egypt. In a bitter twist, God allows his family to be enslaved by a Pharaoh and delivered by a man named Moses.

It's a painful story because no matter how we rationalize it, there is never a good reason for oppression. We get the sense, however, that God allows his children to endure it in Egypt because he wants to teach them early how it feels to be exploited. He wants to teach them, so that as they grow and become more powerful, they will always remember what it was like to be on the bottom. And in remembering this, they will (perhaps) avoid treating others in this manner.

"Remember!" God says over and over. "Remember that you were slaves in Egypt" (see, for example, Deuteronomy 5:15; 15:15; 16:12; 24:18). Remember what it was like for your forefathers there. Remember, so that when the tables turn, and you find yourselves on top, you will know not to treat your brothers and sisters in the ways that you've been treated. Years later, a Jewish Rabbi (Jesus) would even go so far as to say that this way of thinking *sums up* the whole Old Testament. The entirety of the Hebrew Scriptures, boiled down into a single sentence: "Do to others, as you would have them do to you" (Matt. 7:12).

Egypt's lesson is blunt and painful. The rescue operation can begin only when God's family recognizes a reality forgotten by nearly every civilization on the face of the earth: people are more than products. It is a reality forgotten by both the corporate machine and the consumer culture alike. Individuals are more than goods and services! We are (all of us) more than commodities to be used and thrown away. And, ironically, it is a reality that only former slaves can fully grasp. So God allows Israel's children to be enslaved in Egypt. And he allows them to be led out by his grace alone.

Into the Wild

After walking out of oppression without raising so much as a spear, the children of Israel are ushered next into a binding relationship with their Liberator-God. It is a marriage of sorts. It is a *covenant*. The meaning is simple. Based on his faithfulness in the past, God reaffirms his relationship with the children of Israel for the future. Both parties in this marriage are sworn to faithfulness. And just like in a marriage, there are consequences for breaking one's vows. The result is that Israel will be God's people and he will be their God. Other nations will have governmental systems designed to dominate and to destroy, but God's family is to be different. They are to have no King but God himself.

They are to honor God by loving and obeying him. It's a simple concept. But it's not easy. The covenant requires people to remain honest in their dealings, faithful in their marriages, and content with their possessions. They must respect the lives of others, the authority of parents, the property of neighbors, and the name of the one true God who brought them out of slavery. These simple practices form what we call the Ten Commandments.

But even these clear-cut rules are based on something bigger. They are based on a *narrative* of liberation. So before God hands down a single "thou shall not," he reminds them of their story: "I am the LORD your God, who brought you out of Egypt, out of the land of *slavery*" (Deut. 5:6, emphasis mine).

Based on that act of saving grace, God says he wants us to live a different kind of life. He wants us to live a life of love and goodness and worship—a life of honesty, not exploitation. That's the lesson of the Ten Commandments. It's not about rules for the sake of rules. It's about rules for the sake of right relationships. And like everything God does throughout the Bible, it's about communion coming back to the creation.

The Bride and the Bellboy

It's a nice thought. There's something almost quaint about the notion of authentic community making a comeback. But for the children of Israel it seems that trouble starts brewing from almost the first day of their road trip out of Egypt. They have been called to be different, but as most of us discover, being *different* is difficult.

It's a line most of us have heard in the mouth of a child. "But, Mom! Sally's parents say it's okay! Sally's parents let her do it! Sally's parents let her have a pony . . . put on makeup . . . drive at nighttime . . . wear a bikini . . . tattoo the lyrics to Nickelback in Chinese on her lower back . . ." (you get the drift). They used to call it peer pressure, and it stems from the fact that we feel most comfortable when we're doing things pretty much like everybody else. We may say we value independence, but that's mostly because everybody else values it too. In America especially, many "rebels" are just doing what the culture says is cool.

For Israel, the peer pressure shows up in a specific way: the other nations worship idol-kings that they can see and touch. Their gods are visible and their rules are more elastic. The other nations can fight and fornicate whenever it suits them. They can even hedge their religious bets, praying to multiple gods, and thereby increasing the odds that at least one deity will grant their wish. The other nations have kings they can see and hear and put on pedestals. The list goes on and on.

Israel has none of this: no human king, no palace, no temple. And the people grow jealous. What happens next begins a pattern of behavior that crescendos throughout the Old Testament. Just beyond the border of Egypt, the Israelites reject their marriage vows, they reject their covenant, and they begin to behave just like the neighbors. It starts while Moses is still on the mountain with God getting the ten rock rules. In his absence, the people construct an idol—a gaudy golden cow that must have looked like it was designed by the same people who decorate the sets of Christian cable shows.

They make a calf-god. And they worship it. This act of worshipping creation, rather than the Creator, is called idolatry—and it is the great sin of humanity, both then and now. We have been wired to worship at our very core. We will worship. The problem, however, is that we also have a knack for choosing terrible gods. Every sin is just idolatry in one form or another. Yet with the golden calf, the reality is almost too much to grasp. The chosen people have betrayed their marriage vows! And the timing is what's most appalling. Having just left the honeymoon suite, the bride has now committed the spiritual equivalent of bedding the hotel bellboy. It's disgusting. And it leaves us with questions: What will become of Israel now? Will God simply wipe the people out? He did that once with a flood. Will he do it again? Perhaps he wants to.

And yet, he doesn't. This time, the Creator takes an even more daring approach. His people have denied him, yet he refuses to give them up. At the last moment, God remembers his covenant promise to a wrinkled old man named Abraham. And like a jilted lover who can't let go, Yahweh remembers *his* wedding vows. He will stay with his people, and he will keep his promise, even if they have shattered theirs.

Yet there will be consequences. The relationship has changed. And it is at this moment that the Creator takes creative action. If Israel will not stand out *morally* then she will stand out in another way. She will stand out physically and culturally. In other words, if the old covenant did not change the people's hearts, then it must at least change their appearance. Israel must be *set apart* in order to survive among the neighbors.[7]

In this way, the Creator will preserve his people until the day when an Israel (or an Israelite) can come along and embody the life that will show the world what God is really like. And with this creative twist, we begin to understand one reason for some of the strangest passages in the entire Bible.

What's "Cud" Got to Do with It?

After the incident with the golden calf, the biblical text is littered with what modern folks might see as some of the most peculiar rules imaginable. In books like Leviticus and Deuteronomy, the loving Creator we meet in the beginning appears to morph into what might seem like a legalistic schoolmaster with a touch of OCD.

There are meticulous rules on almost everything. Strange rules! And it's for this reason that most Christians simply ignore these sections of the Bible. The commands seem foreign and legalistic. "Don't touch this! Don't eat this! Don't put these two kinds of fabric together!" The list goes on and on.

There are even rules on what foods to eat. Cud chewers are good. Animals with split hooves are good. But then it gets complicated. Take the rabbit. Apparently, he chews his cud. But he's got no hooves. So he's off-limits. Thou shalt not eat rabbit! Or take the pig: she's got split hooves, but she doesn't chew her cud. So she's out too. Take one bite of pork tenderloin, and you might as well have clubbed a cocker spaniel (see Leviticus 11:1–9).

All these rules eventually raise the question that Tina Turner never got around to. That is, when it comes to religion, What's *cud* got to do with it? What's cud have to do with anything?! Why should God care if someone has a pork chop or some rabbit stew? What do these strange rules have to do with spirituality?

Christians have given all kinds of creative answers to this question. Some claim that Yahweh is protecting his people from health risks associated with such foods. Perhaps some of them were. Ironically, however, almost none of these people seem to find such risks reason enough to adopt a similar diet themselves!

Others claim that these laws were given in an effort to keep Israel away from pagan rituals that were associated with such practices. Ironically though, God seems to have no problem with other practices—say, eating the meat of bulls or drinking wine—which were much more commonly used in pagan rites. So in the end, this theory seems incomplete as well.

So we are back where we started. What's cud have to do with anything? What do these peculiar rules have to do with spirituality? Perhaps the most important explanation is the one that we've already mentioned. It seems that many of these strange rules have to do with *preserving* a distinct people—a people who are set apart from the surrounding nations—and not with *propagating* a bizarre religious legalism. I'll try to explain.

Culture Matters

The Christian God was never the legalistic father that some have made him out to be. He was never an angry schoolmaster who imposed meaningless legalisms just because it suited him. In fact, these rules were never God's chief desire at all. His ultimate desire was for Israel to stand out because of her mercy, fidelity, and love. He wanted her to love him, and in doing so, to love people in ways that led to flourishing and shalom. He wanted her to remember the fatherless and the widow, and to value every human life because she had seen the effects of treating people like products.

But because his family refused to stand out in this way, the Creator chose to graciously preserve his people by other methods. As any anthropologist can tell you, a culture *must* possess elements unique to itself if it is to have any hope of survival. (Those reading this who are immigrants will know exactly what I'm talking about.) If a minority group simply adopts the lifestyle of its majority neighbors, then it ceases to exist as a unique culture. For God's family to survive, they must be set apart in noticeable ways.

If Israel would be no different from her neighbors spiritually and morally, then she must be different outwardly and culturally. In this way, the God of Abraham would sustain his family until a point when Someone could come along to live out the *heart* of the commandments.

Until that time, however, the unique laws of the Old Testament preserved the calling and identity of Israel in the same way that other cultures have been sustained for thousands of years.[8] Later on, in the New Testament, we will be given an indication of which commands still apply, and which ones have run their course. But, for now, it is time to leave the wilderness. It's on to the promised land!

The Bible and Marie Antoinette

Several years ago, my wife and I made our sacred pilgrimage to a shrine called Movie Gallery. For younger readers, this is a long-forgotten place of commerce where old people used to rent movies and TV shows before Netflix, Amazon, and the internet. We rode there in our covered wagon.

Unfortunately, on this occasion, I walked out holding a bright pink DVD case for a movie dubiously titled *Marie Antoinette*. Hilarity did not ensue.

In case you're not a History Channel junkie, Marie Antoinette was the last queen of France before the great Revolution (about the same time as America's) in which starving French citizens decided to take liberty into their own hands. Eventually, in a period called The Terror, they built a giant sausage slicer called the guillotine. They used the device to lop off royal craniums like the leafy ends of carrots. It was a bloody business and needless to say, things didn't end well for Marie. But the movie wasn't about her death. The movie was primarily about the way Marie and her royal entourage *lived* before the revolution.

Here's a synopsis: they lived well.

While French peasants starved, Marie (or at least the movie version) partied like a Hollywood celebrity. Every night was a red-carpet affair, and every day was filled with weighty decisions like which shade of pink fabric should adorn the royal poodles.

You know, important stuff.

In the film, she was the Paris Hilton of Paris, and almost as well-spoken. History remembers her primarily for her supposed response to the news that French citizens were starving without bread. Marie's humanitarian solution would thus become as famous as she: "No bread?" she asked. "Let them eat cake!" It seemed simple enough. (Spoiler alert: the real Marie Antionette may not have ever said that.)

The ironic thing about the movie was the way in which the director went to great pains to show that Marie wasn't *really* a bad person. She wasn't *really* malicious. She hadn't asked to be queen. She didn't even want the job. She was pushed into it.

The director's point was simple. Marie wasn't evil per se. Marie was just living out the part of a queen within that decadent and tone-deaf chapter of French history. She was living like a *royal*. But as it often does, the unrestricted freedom given to the powerful only served to cut her off from the concerns of the common people starving in the streets of Paris. Marie's position distanced her from the realities of regular Joes (or Pierres), and it led to her demise.

There's a name for this phenomenon. The Old Testament scholar Walter Brueggeman sees the scenario as a natural result of what he calls "the royal consciousness." And he sees it in Israel's history too.[9]

A Royal Mess

After exiting the wilderness for the promised land, an unsettling reality becomes apparent for God's people. Despite their best efforts, not even lengthy law codes are enough to protect them from the constant desire to be more like the pagan neighbors. They are commanded to *drive out* their enemies, but this is difficult when one envies them.[10] The Israelites want more than a covenant to define them; they want a king. So God gives them what they want. But this concession comes with a dire warning.

This is what will happen. God says: While your precious king grows rich, your babies will grow hungry. While your queen picks pricey fabric, you'll pick which mouth to feed. Your sons will be drafted to fight wars; your daughters will be taken as perfumers; your fields and flocks will be ravaged by taxation. And then, after a long list of woes, there comes the kicker: "you yourselves will become his slaves" (see 1 Samuel 8:11–17).

With the royal consciousness comes a return to Egypt-like existence. And it will be this way, God says, because no matter how noble its beginning, every earthly kingdom ends with the same agenda. It is what the royal consciousness is all about. It's about *maintaining power at any price.* "You want a king," God says. "Alright, but it's going to cost you." And it does.

For the remainder of their stay in the land of Canaan, the children of Israel struggle under the guidance of kings either too greedy, too proud, or too stupid to shepherd a people. There are bright spots, of course. There is a Cinderella story of a shepherd-king named David, a Renaissance man who expands Israel's borders, strengthens her faith, and pens a songbook for the ages. But even with David, seeds of destruction are being sown. Taxes are raised, integrity is bartered, and blood is spilled in bucket loads.

Behind the scenes, things continue to decline under David's son. Though bright beyond measure, Solomon is born with a silver spoon in hand. While beginning with more wisdom than the world ever knew, he ends his reign as Israel's brilliant fool. And his extravagance has consequences. A subversive commentary on Solomon's indulgence (sexual, economic, and otherwise) is recorded by the writer of a book called 2 Chronicles. When given the task of recording the king's annual salary, the scribe writes down this very specific number (I feel like I've heard of it somewhere before . . .): "The weight of the gold that Solomon received yearly was 666 talents" (2 Chron. 9:13).

To even the casual reader, or the casual watcher of *The Exorcist,* the message in the numbers now seems clear: 666 is what happens when earthly rulers go too far. Their reign becomes demonic and oppressive. They become part of what the New Testament calls "the principalities and powers" (see Ephesians 6).

For God's people, the reality was clear. The kings Yahweh never wanted were leading Israel down a path of no return. And Solomon was just the beginning. After him, the kingdom was split by civil war, and things went from bad to worse.

Through a royal parade of bumbling monarchs, the Jewish nation descended into idolatry and exploitation. Instead of caring for the widow, the orphan and the foreigner, they exploited common people for common profit. Like modern televangelists, they turned true religion (a phrase from the New Testament book of James)[11] into yet another means to take advantage. They exacted exorbitant taxes, distorted the Scriptures, and ran rackets in God's name.[12]

The result was sad and sickening. The family that was supposed to show the world what God was like had become a part of the problem. Eventually God's patience wore thin, and it was time for yet another road trip. Israel would be driven from their promised land by foreign armies. They would go into exile, and it would be there that they would learn a painful lesson. Idolatry and oppression have horrific consequences.

Prophets: God's Megaphones

Yet as the exilic road trip lurched ever closer, there were also signs that God was not finished with his family. Amid the commotion of the royal mess, there were other sounds emerging—sounds of *voices* crying out, as it were, in the wilderness. The voices belonged to God's prophets. The prophets were megaphones of truth in a culture that was hard of hearing. We'll close Israel's chapter by listening to them.

As we come to the end of the Hebrew Scriptures, we encounter these ragged wild-eyed figures. Prophets. For some of us, the very word brings to mind a kind of fortune teller. But in the Old Testament, the prophets are not so much the seers of the distant future, as the tellers of the painful truth. They are thorns in the side of the royal consciousness. And they are the means by which God chooses to speak to his dysfunctional family. The prophets are the slightly crazy ones who dare to stare a pip-squeak ruler in the face and remind him that there is a greater King to be obeyed.

They have eccentric Hebrew names befitting of their character—names like Isaiah, Ezekiel, Obadiah, Habakkuk, and Zephaniah. Unbowed by idols and unimpressed with royal opulence, these men and women emerge at various times to remind God's wayward rescuers of their true calling. "We were called to be the light of the world!" they say. "We were called to bless the nations and restore community to creation!" Some weep, some shout, and some wear strange clothes. But in all their imaginative eccentricity, the overriding prophetic message is a simple one: repent!

Admittedly, it is a message that most of us do not like hearing. It is a message associated with wild-eyed street preachers, or Bible-thumping fundamentalists. It has an edge and it carries an accusation. Yet with the prophets, the accusation is well-founded. God was coming to judge his family. In the year 722 BC, the Assyrian military swept into Canaan and wiped the northern tribes of Israel off the map. They would scarcely be heard from again.

Then, in 586 BC, the remaining southern tribe of Judah—the tribe of the shepherd-king—would face a similar fate, this time at the hands of Babylon. The foreigners swooped in like vultures, killing many, and carrying the best and brightest off to exile.

The prophets' warnings had come true. For more than a generation God's family would languish in a foreign land. They would weep and mourn. But more importantly, they would repent. They would come clean of their idolatry and many would commit themselves to the laws that God had given them. Then, after more than a generation away, some would be allowed to trickle back into their burned-out homeland. Books like Haggai, Zechariah, and Malachi were written during this slow return.

When All Seemed Hopeless

But despite returning *physically* to the land, in many ways, exile continued. A third-rate temple was erected on the site of Solomon's monstrosity. But God's presence often seemed strangely absent. While some rejoiced at the moral victory, others wept because the new building was an embarrassment compared to the old. For the Israelites, their World Trade Center had been demolished, only to be replaced by a two-story duplex. It was disheartening, and for most, the sad reality was obvious: the pagans had won.

The great prophecies of renewal remained unful-filled.[13] In most cases, the idol-worshipping foreigners were still in charge. And the people of God had been humiliated. From the time of their return to the land, until the end of the Old Testament, the Jewish people would subsist mostly under the boot of foreign kings and foreign armies. Never again would they command their land in the manner of the shepherd-king. They had been embarrassed, and this embarrassment raised questions.

How would God's original promise to a wrinkled old man named Abram be fulfilled? How would the nations of the earth be blessed through this beaten band of nobodies? Had Yahweh forgotten his people? Had he finally had enough? Was it ridiculous to think that rescue could come through a dysfunctional family like that of Israel? For years the questions went unanswered.

Then, just when all seemed hopeless, something unexpected happened in a forgotten corner of the Roman Empire. Just when all seemed lost, finally there was reason to be optimistic. In a nothing-town called Nazareth, an unmarried teenage girl got pregnant. And the world would never be the same.

Engage the Story

Having read about the Israel chapter in God's Story, it's time now to engage with it yourself. Read the following passages this week, reflect upon their meaning, and be prepared to discuss them with others:

- Genesis 12:1–9 (The call of Abraham)
- Exodus 3 (The call of Moses)
- Exodus 19–20 (The giving of the Law at Sinai)

- 2 Samuel 7 (The Lord's covenant with David)
- Isaiah 6 (The call of Isaiah)
- Psalm 137 (The lament of the exiles)

Discuss the Story

1. The third chapter in the biblical storyline is about a rescue operation begun by God to restore shalom to his fallen creation. Yet God doesn't go about fixing our world in the way we might expect. He doesn't send a superhero, or a politician, or a celebrity. Instead he uses a beautiful and dysfunctional family—kind of like yours.

   - Why do you think God chooses unlikely people to do his work? What benefit might this have?
   - Read Genesis 12:1–2 aloud together and use it to discuss the following questions:
     What does God say that Abram's descendants will do *for* the nations?
     How might this passage have implications for how we are called to serve those outside the church?

2. Israel is the most commonly used name for God's family. The name itself refers to those who wrestle with God.

   - How is the name Israel a fitting title for God's family? How does it describe their calling as a people? How does it apply to *our* calling?

- The chapter argues that "Jacob" was more than just a name; it was also a label. Have you ever had to deal with a negative label that was attached to you—either by others or by yourself? How so?
- Throughout the Scriptures God has a way of changing the hurtful labels associated with his children. Have you experienced this in your own life? How has God changed a hurtful label attached to you?

3. Years after Abraham, Isaac, and Jacob, God's family ends up stuck as slaves in Egypt. It is here that they become a nation.

- What should the years spent in slavery have taught God's family about how they were to treat others? Why does God constantly call them to "remember" this time (see Deuteronomy 5:15; 15:15; 16:12; 24:18)?
- The chapter argues that one move toward slavery is any behavior that treats people like products. Have you experienced this in your own life? Have you ever been made to feel like a product? Have you ever treated others this way? How so?
- Take a moment to discuss the statement below:

Egypt's lesson is blunt and painful. From the very beginning, God makes clear that the rescue operation can begin only when his children recognize a reality forgotten by nearly every civilization on the face of the planet: people are more than products. It is a reality forgotten by both the corporate machine and the consumer culture alike: individuals are more than goods and services! We are (all of us) more than products. And ironically, perhaps it is a reality that only former slaves can fully grasp.

4. Perhaps the most important event in the Old Testament occurs when God leads his family *out* of Egypt, *through* the wilderness, and *toward* the promised land. It is at the beginning of this journey that God's people receive some commands (the Ten Commandments) to guide their behavior. Unfortunately, Moses hardly has time to deliver these commands before the people knowingly break God's covenant. Read Exodus 32:1–4 to refresh your memory of this story.

   • In what ways did Israel give in to the pressure to be like the neighbors?
   • In what ways do you give in to this same pressure?
   • Israel's archetypal sin was idolatry; what person or thing in your life can most easily become an idol?

5. Shortly after the Israelites reject God in the wilderness, we begin to be confronted with page after page of very specific laws. Read the statement below and reflect on the questions to follow:

   There are meticulous rules on almost everything! Some seem very strange, and it is for this reason that many Christians simply ignore these sections of the Bible. The commands seem foreign and legalistic. "Don't touch this! Don't eat this! Don't put these two kinds of fabric together!" The list goes on and on.

- What is one of God's purposes in handing down *some* of the most meticulous and obscure rules in the Old Testament?
- Have you ever thought of the God of the Old Testament as a kind of legalistic schoolmaster? What is wrong with this perspective?
- What does it mean to say that God used many of these commands to preserve (set apart) a culture, *not* to propound legalism?

6. Even after settling in the promised land, it becomes clear that God's family is far from perfect. Through a succession of wicked leaders and wayward followers, the wrestlers still need rescuing. The family that was to be the bringer of God's solution has instead become a part of the problem.

- How does this same thing happen in our own lives? How do we become a part of the problem rather than a part of the solution to sin and suffering in our world?

The prophets were God's megaphones to his wayward family. Read Micah 6:6–8 together and spend some time in closing this week asking God how you can become a part of the solution to the brokenness of the world around you.

JESUS

Why Directors Should Wear Makeup

Several years ago, some friends and I ventured out to the local Cineplex to see a movie by a young director named M. Night Shyamalan. I was going, in part, because someone had told me that "M. Night" was going to be the next Alfred Hitchcock. (If you have followed his career path since then, you know that this did *not* prove true. Like, at all. But I digress.) At the time, I had never seen a Hitchcock movie, but I pretended to be impressed.

I don't remember much about the film itself, but as we drove to the theater I do remember someone mentioning that one of Shyamalan's trademarks was to cast himself as a kind of minor character in many of his films. In other words, he wasn't content to write or direct a particular movie; he also wanted to find a way into the script. He wanted to be *in it*, if only for a moment.

And I suppose that's understandable. After all, it is one thing to yell "Cut!" and write dialogue and position cameras, but it's quite another thing to be *in* the movie. It's something else entirely to get up from your fancy director's chair, set down your clipboard (I imagine directors with clipboards), and step into the story. It's one thing to direct, but it's quite another thing to cake on the makeup of an actor and play a part.

Strange as it sounds, this is precisely the sort of thing that Christians believe took place with the out-of-wedlock birth of a baby boy named Jesus. In Jesus, the Scriptures claim that the Author of God's Story, the Director himself, got up from his cushy seat and stepped into the plotline. In Jesus, the Master Painter set down his brush, and quietly strode onto the blood-and-paint-smeared canvas.[1] The Artist took up residence within the artwork.

Yet the question we must answer in this chapter pertains more to what *difference* this brief appearance actually makes. Was Jesus little more than an extra on the movie screen of human history—a brief blip on the radar? Or was he more? Was his incarnation merely a divine cameo in an otherwise tragic plotline? Or was it something greater? *What difference does this Jesus make in the way our movie ends?* This is the question on which the entire story hinges.

But before attempting to answer, perhaps we should start the Jesus-chapter where God starts it. Not with grandiose religious theories, or high-flown rhetoric, but with a trembling teenage girl, alone and pregnant.

Birth: The Plastic Paperweight

When I was still in my youthful early twenties, I took some time on a frigid December evening to do something I have never done. After dinner with Brianna, I put on my fake cow-hide coat, left the warmth of our apartment, and set out on a mission.

After a couple minutes of white-knuckled driving, I parked our teal Chevy Cavalier outside the neighborhood Walgreens, rummaged the glove box for a cyanide capsule (in case things went south), and walked nervously into the glare of fluorescent lighting and the familiar trills of Kenny G *The Holiday Album*. (Retail stores are required by law to play Kenny G's Christmas records. It's a conspiracy, and I have my theory as to what dark lord is behind it.)

This was it.

Upon entering, I scanned the store for anyone I might know—anyone from church or the gym. No one looked familiar. But you can never be too sure. Walgreens is full of hiding places. You never know when someone might pop up like a jack-in-the-box from behind the makeup counter. I fingered the cyanide. Then I swallowed hard, conjured the *mojo* of Jack Bauer, and headed for the one aisle I had always avoided. It's the aisle that strikes fear in every red-blooded American male. It's the aisle with the female accoutrements.

In a few seconds, I brushed past an assortment of unknown products until finding myself face-to-face with a series of shelves auspiciously labeled: "Home Pregnancy Tests." Was I really doing this?

After gathering my courage, I suddenly realized a problem that I had never expected. There are precisely 467 different kinds of home pregnancy tests, each with a compelling medical argument for why that device is the scientifically superior product for you to pee on.

I felt my cheeks getting hot. Just then a woman shuffled past me. I could read her expression. *You poor boy,* she was thinking, *your life is about to get so complicated.* That was the clincher. My hand shot out like a lizard tongue and I grabbed the closest test I could get my fingers on. I gave the mystery lady the fake smile I used in my senior pictures, and I beat it for the checkout. I paid cash and left with the words of an ex-president ringing in my ears: mission accomplished.

That week I wrote out our church's Christmas sermon with the world's strangest paperweight sitting on the corner of my desk. You might say it was my *inspiration.* After unwrapping the little plastic stick, I placed it just to the right of my laptop. Then I proceeded to reread the stories of Jesus' birth.

In reality, Brianna and I were not (yet) pregnant, and we never thought we were. I had purchased the magic wand for another reason. I bought it because for some reason I needed a tangible reminder that amid the happiness of the holiday season—the recycled Kenny G and the children's plays with blue bathrobes—a grittier reality undergirds the Christmas story. It's the reality of an unplanned pregnancy and an unplanned Visitor. That's why I bought the test. I needed the plastic paperweight to remind me of what it might be like for a shell-shocked teenager to stare down at the double pink lines and wonder: *How in the world am I going to explain this?*

Royal Birth, Royal Scandal

The mother of Jesus could relate to this question. As a Jewish girl in the first century, Mary would have known the punishment for such supposed *indiscretions*. She could be legally executed. And it was a possibility that might loom larger should the small-town rumor mill suggest that it was a Roman soldier, and not a Hebrew boyfriend, who was behind it. This wasn't a story for a greeting card. Things looked bad for Mary. In a small town, she would be doomed to a life as the black sheep with the bastard baby.

And with this gritty reality, we glimpse the paradox that marks the beginning of the Jesus chapter: two themes set side by side. We are told *first* that this event will be a *royal birth*, the birth of a king. And at the same time, we told also of a *royal scandal*. This child's birth will give rise to rumors of the kind that travel faster than a brushfire. Two realities, laid side by side:

Royal birth.

Royal scandal.

In Luke's gospel, the words of the angel hint at both. While Mary sits quivering from the shock of an angelic visitor, God's messenger delivers a news flash: You will get pregnant before sex and before marriage. You will give birth to a boy and his name will be Jesus:

> "He will be great and will be called the Son of the Most High. The Lord God will give him the

throne of his father David, and he will reign over Jacob's descendants forever; his kingdom will never end." (Luke 1:32–33)

His *kingdo*m. There is the reminder. This is to be a royal birth. But it is couched in royal scandal.

And as the pregnancy plays out, the two themes continue. The local despot, Herod the Great, hears the royal rumor and acts decisively. Kingly gossip must be quashed, and Herod—who would kill both sons and wives for less—is hardly squeamish. Bethlehem becomes a bloodbath. Royal birth. Royal scandal.

Later, court astrologers (Magi) come from kingdoms in the East. They are looking for a child whose birth has produced the kind of night-sky pyrotechnics usually reserved for Roman Caesars. (Translation: they have seen a star.) And for the ancients, stars did more than twinkle. For the ancients, stars screamed royal messages: "Take heed! The old order is changing! A new King has been born!"

Because this was the meaning of the star, it was only natural to bring gifts, not for a baby shower, but for the coronation of a new crown prince. It was a rogue coronation, like the one the prophet Samuel held for David. It was the kind of baby shower that could get you killed; and for Jesus, it almost does.

Jesus' family flees to Egypt. But even this road trip serves to underscore the royal birth and scandal. For the family of Abraham, the symbolism was hardly subtle. Egypt was the ancient land of slavery, the land where Yahweh heard his people cry and led them out of bondage. So for all who heard of Jesus' flight to the nation of the Nile, the meaning was clear: the would-be king was retracing the steps of men like Moses and Joshua. He was reliving Israel's story, but with fidelity. The trip to Egypt was an exodus in miniature. It was an exile, followed by return. The crown prince was taking on the role of his ancient forefathers. In time, he would leave Egypt for the promised land, and for all who later heard of this, the next step would seem obvious: first comes exodus; then comes *conquest*.

In other words, there was going to be a fight. For all who heard the tale of the special baby born in Bethlehem, this stark conclusion would remain the overriding take-away. From the manger forward, all the tension builds toward this conclusion. You cannot have two kings. You cannot have two masters. *There was going to be a fight*.

Shakespeare could have told us this. And, in a way, the beginning of the Jesus chapter reads like a Shakespearian play. It reads a bit like *Macbeth* or *Hamlet*. There are rival claims to kingship, and as Shakespeare knew well, rival claims can end in only one way. At the end of the play, someone (or more likely, many someones) must lay dead. At the end of the story, either Caesar, or Herod, or Jesus himself must lie in a pool of cooling blood. That's how these stories always end. There *was* going to be a fight. That's the dark shadow behind the Christmas story.

Yet as we leave the royal birth and scandal of Jesus' birth, we are left with questions: When will this fight take place? What will it look like? And who will win? These are the crucial questions, but they can be answered only by a look forward into Jesus' adult life and ministry.

Meeting Mac

Somewhere in the middle of my own transition into adulthood, I met Mac. I remember it because it was the beginning of my first semester in a new school on the East Coast. At the time, I was standing by the day-old lettuce in the cafeteria salad bar, holding a plastic tray, and trying not to relive bad memories from junior high. (You know the ones. *Dear God, please let me sit with the cool kids.* It's proof we're all born sinful.) I was twenty-two years old but somehow that nause-ated feeling of the first day of school was still tucked beneath my ribcage.

To be honest, I've never been good with mingling. While speaking in front of several hundred people is no big deal, having to actually converse with human creatures makes me anxious. And I'm even worse when it comes to meeting new people, which explains why I spent the previous week's mealtimes sequestered in my dorm with a fridge of TV dinners. But I was here now, by the day-old lettuce, and it was time to be social.

About this time, I noticed a guy in the oversized red T-shirt sitting in the corner of the room. It was Mac, but I didn't know it yet. All I knew was that the people at his table seemed to be enjoying themselves. So with a deep breath I said good-bye to the lettuce, pulled up a plastic chair, and was sucked into a conversation that would continue for the next two years.

It didn't take many lunches to realize Mac was one of the most quick-witted people I had ever met. He was hilarious, and people were drawn to him. I think most of us know someone like that, someone who could have done stand-up comedy or *The Daily Show*. Mac was like that.

Then there was the T-shirt. He seemed to always have it on. Or perhaps he owned one for every day of the week. It was red, a little faded, and it had only one thing on it. Right in middle of the front side, was a larger than life portrait of one Ernesto "Che" Guevara.

I had to pretend at first to know who Che was. I thought initially that he looked a little like a grown-up version of Benny "the Jet" Rodriguez from *The Sandlot*. But that didn't explain the communist beret. Benny would never wear that. The truth was, I didn't have a clue about Che. But judging by the hat and the big red Commie star, I was pretty sure he wasn't Ronald Reagan's younger brother Roy.

The portrait on the shirt showed a man with a scruffy beard, a proud square jaw, and an implacable far-off expression. He looked a like a young Fidel Castro, which, to a conservative kid from Kansas, was a little disconcerting.

I later learned that Che was a Marxist revolutionary. He was, in essence, a Communist insurgent. Yet to his followers, Guevara was a freedom fighter. To admirers, Che was a Robin Hood who moved through forgotten parts of the world, planting seeds of political change. To most Americans, he was little more than a violent and murderous thug. Opinions varied.

I never learned how Mac *really* felt about Che. I suspect that he wore the shirt partly just to mess with conservative faculty members who might get ruffled when they saw the rebel leader walking proudly around their evangelical seminary. Yet as I began to read some of the varying accounts of Guevara's life, I found that even his enemies had to admit that he was a compelling leader. People were drawn to him, partly because he had left a comfortable life as a doctor to adopt the precarious existence of a revolutionary. His movement grew, and by his early thirties the CIA was actively plotting to kill him. The fear was that his violent Marxist tendencies would open the way for a communist foothold throughout the developing world. And for the United States, this was *no bueno*. A dictator could be paid off, but someone like Guevara was another story.

Che was a marked man, and by 1967 he was tracked down and killed while leading a violent revolution in Bolivia. To this day the questions and rumors about his life continue to swirl. Some see him as a hero, others as a violent crackpot; some as a modern Robin Hood, others as an *Al Qaeda*-like insurgent. Opinions still vary.

Whatever the true nature of Che's legacy (and I am hardly one of his fan boys), the fact remains that to his followers, the man on the T-shirt offered something many of us take for granted. He offered ordinary people an opportunity to be a part of a decisive movement, a revolution, to turn the tables on the way it's always been and make way for a new future in which even the nobodies could be a part.[2] That's what revolutionaries have always offered. And that's where Jesus of Nazareth comes in.

A Revolutionary Life

Unfortunately, many of us have been led to think of Jesus in ways that hide the revolutionary nature of his life. This happens in two ways. On the one hand, the secular culture has led us to think of grown-up Jesus as a kind of a first-century Oprah. He was a compassionate if somewhat effeminate man who delivered good advice and tried to help people. According to some portraits, he spent much of his time cuddling baby lambs and offering a gospel of warm fuzzies to a world with low self-esteem.

For evidence of this view we need only look to polls showing that while the general public *strongly* dislikes the church, they're still *ga-ga* for Jesus. Some writers use these statistics to prove that the church is chock-full of mean-spirited fundamentalists. There are some of these to be sure. But the stats on Jesus' popularity probably reveal more of the way in which he has become a blank canvas onto which we project whatever qualities we find personally appealing. For the culture, Jesus is one cardigan shy of a first-century Mr. Rogers. He's *nice*. But then again, nice people don't normally get themselves executed for crimes against the state.

In other words, Oprah-Jesus never existed.

On the opposite extreme, we've been led by some in the church to think of Jesus' life in purely spiritual terms. He was, from this perspective, a kind of benevolent ticket scalper, dispensing free passes to the afterlife. He was a spiritual real-estate developer selling heavenly McMansions someplace north of Del Boca Vista. For this

Jesus, the goal was simple: he *came* to earth so we can *leave* it—and go to heaven when we die. End of story.

But as with the Jesus of pop culture, there are problems with this Jesus too. One problem emerges when we notice that the Jesus of Scripture spends much of his time talking about what it would look like for the kingdom of heaven to come *here,* not *up there* in Del Boca Vista. He prayed: "Thy kingdom come, on earth as it is in heaven."

In other words, the Jesus of Scripture wasn't just selling heavenly condos, he was also sparking a this-world revolution. That's why most of his messages describe what it looks like when God's kingdom takes root among us. The Jesus of Scripture said it this way: *the kingdom of God* is like this:

> It's like a *mustard seed*, starting small but growing large. (see Mark 4:30–32)
>
> It's like a *priceless pearl*, worth giving all to possess. (see Matthew 13:45–46)[3]
>
> It's like a *net*, that separates good fish from bad. (see Matthew 13:47–49)

This is the nature of the kingdom. It's cryptic. Yet one thing is clear. In a land that *already* had a king (Caesar, Herod, etc.), new kingdom talk was very, very dangerous. New kingdom talk was new king talk and while it could get you followers, it could also get you killed.

In many ways, new kingdom talk is the message mouthed by revolutionaries across the centuries. It was the message of people like Che Guevara, Thomas Jefferson, and William Wallace—*but with one crucial difference!* Instead of encouraging his followers to take up arms, the rebel Lord from Nazareth was encouraging an even more radical uprising. Now a word on that.

Parables on CNN

When I'm working (as I am now) on my laptop, I can easily minimize this document and move to something called the internet. (Or as a former U.S. president put it: the *intra-nets*.) And once on the *intra-nets,* I can check or send an e-mail, order something off of Amazon, or, as I do more frequently, I can check the headlines.

Unfortunately, when I do check the headlines, I am usually greeted by a particular kind of image: the image of the battlefield. A car bomb in Riyadh, an IED in Baghdad, a suicide bomber on the West Bank. There are atrocities too numerous to count, some of which originate not far from the Middle Eastern landscape where Jesus walked and taught. Indeed, one might even suppose after viewing the news that although much has changed since the Author stepped into the story, many things remain the same. Sectarian violence belongs firmly in the latter category.

And so it is while viewing the headlines that we are forced to marvel again at the revolutionary message of Jesus.

We marvel because from the moment his life began it seemed that Jesus was destined for a fight. The birth stories tell us this much, and his ministry reinforces the feeling. It begins with his baptism and symbolic crossing of the Jordan River (the same river crossed by the Old

Testament warrior *Joshua*—whose name in the Greek is identical to that of Jesus). It continues as he calls twelve disciples (one for each tribe that conquered the Canaanites). And it climaxes with a ministry that centers on the coming of the so-called kingdom of God.

The miracles, the prophecies, the pointed parables— all seemed to be signs that the violent day of the Lord was finally at hand. And on this day, *there was going to be a fight*. Revolution was at hand, and what else could this be but the run-up to the final battle in which the Messiah would drive out the pagans and reclaim the land? This was it! Soon the new *Joshua* would honor his violent namesake. The Son of the shepherd-king would rally his mighty men, blood would flow, and embarrassed foreigners would stream to Jerusalem to learn the Torah and become repentant Jewish converts (see Jeremiah 3:14–17).

And yet . . . almost as quickly as this hope emerges, the unpredictable Rabbi starts going off the revolutionary reservation. He starts saying things that bring the nature of the movement into question. Things like: love your enemies, turn your cheek, and pray for those who persecute you (see Matthew 5:39, 44). He starts talking about how he is going to die, and what is worse, he starts criticizing the religious do-gooders and hanging out with sinners! This is not what was expected.

Beards and Kilts

To grasp how bizarre Jesus' behavior must have seemed, you might imagine a scene from the old Mel Gibson movie *Braveheart*. In this scene, you see William Wallace racing back and forth on horseback, in front of his army. (And you know it's him because, let's be honest, only one guy wears blue face paint like a medieval Smurf.) But this time, instead of giving a rousing pep talk that would make even a suburban basement-dweller go out and buy a kilt, Wallace takes a different course. This time, you hear Mel Gibson's quasi-Scottish accent say something like: "You've heard it said, 'love your countrymen and hate the *British*.' But I tell you: love the *British* and pray for them!"[4]

End of speech. Cue the Celtic whistle thing.

Of course, in the original version, this is where all the Beards and Skirts start cheering and waving weapons like half-soused Raiders fans. But in the revised version—the one you're watching now—that doesn't happen. In the revised version, the guys in beards in skirts just stare at Smurf-face on his big dumb horse. They just gawk at him in eerie silence. Then a single brogue-ish voice yells the question everyone is thinking: "What the heck was that?! I thought we came to fight!"

I picture the Jewish Zealots asking Jesus a similar question. "I thought you brought us here to fight?! You've been talking of a new kingdom on earth, as it is in heaven. So what's all this psycho-babble about loving your enemies and letting them kill you?!" Peter asks a question like this, to which Christ promptly calls him Satan—something Oprah-Jesus would never do (see Matthew 16:23).

In the end, we're all left wondering along with the crowds and the disciples and the guys in beards and kilts: Where did this revolution go wrong? How could the man with the royal birth and the revolutionary life *not* do what everyone expected? How could he not raise an army, storm the gates, and usher in God's kingdom? How could he say and do so much, only to walk away from the battlefield like a yellow-bellied coward? The sentiment of Peter's question hangs like a pall over the end of Jesus' ministry: we thought there was going to be a fight!

Of course, if you've read the New Testament, you know a fight is coming. By the end of Jesus' life, blood will spill and soldiers will do what soldiers have been trained to do. There will be a fight. But it won't look like anything George Washington or Che Guevara or William Wallace would have expected. Because in *this* story, the battle is won by a naked, groaning Jew, who is hammered to a Roman cross.

Death—It's Bad

This is perhaps the most important part of God's whole Story. But before addressing the crucifixion, we need to identify a basic theological truth. Get ready for it. Here it is: *death is bad*. Profound, right? Yet true. Folks can write poetry about its inevitability or wax eloquent by couching it in songs or eulogies, but when it comes down to it—in the Bible—death is *bad*. End of story. Paul calls it the final enemy (see 1 Corinthians 15:26). And, in case you're wondering, enemies are bad too.

This truth came home for me with crushing force a few years ago when I stood next to the bed of my brother-in-law and watched him die. Daniel was only thirty. He was funny, young, and handsome. He was a loving husband to my youngest sister, who is perhaps the strongest person I know. They were still newlyweds. His death, and the terrible decline that preceded it, are the worst things I have ever witnessed. ALS is insidious. And despite endless ice buckets dumped on countless heads, no cure exists.

Watching Daniel die changed me. And while I have no claim to the depth of grief borne by his more immediate family, his passing stole some measure of my innocence. In movies, death is valorized and sanitized, but there is one thing the films get wrong: death's color. On screen, the deceased look like they are merely sleeping. But Daniel did not look like that. While he died painlessly, I could not join others in kissing his face, holding his hands, or stroking his hair. I just wanted to get out of there—to flee the room, avert my gaze, cover up his body—anything to escape the pallor that had replaced his former complexion. The image scarred me. For as the theologian John Zizioulas writes: "There is no greater contradiction than a dying being."

That is why I wriggled uncomfortably in my chair last month as I heard a graduation speaker (and pastor) affirm the words of the late Steve Jobs: "Death is very likely the single best invention of Life. It is Life's change agent. It clears out the old to make way for the new."

This may sound nice at first, but when applied to actual people—a son or daughter, a spouse or friend— it is insulting and absurd. It is wrong because it treats human beings like excess inventory at a used car lot. *Act now! Older models must go!* Death is not Life's best creation, and while Jobs said it, he didn't actually believe it. If he had, he would not have fought so furiously (and valiantly) to fend off this great "invention."

For those who mourn—and there are many—such platitudes don't wash against the image of a departed loved one. The bony hand of death cannot be manicured. It is always ugly, always cold, always an offense. While we are often glad to know that a loved one is no longer suffering, it is not death we celebrate; it is the cessation of pain, and their presence with God. Death remains an enemy combatant. It is an intruder into God's good world. It's bad.

So the obvious question is: Why would Jesus' death be any different? Why would a violent execution be good news to anybody? What makes Jesus' death any more beneficial than say, the senseless snuffing out of teenage life along a lonely highway? Why don't we immortalize that scene in tiny 14-carat artwork—the last second before the two cars collide, on a dainty silver necklace? Why don't rappers tattoo *that* scene on their biceps? What is it about the cross that is so singular that it forms the pulsing, hope-filled center of God's Story?

The most obvious answer is that Jesus' death was *temporary*. Jesus' death, you might say, *didn't stick*. He came back. According to the Scriptures, Jesus didn't stay dead, and that makes him at least unique. But to answer the question like this is really to avoid an answer. It is to simply skip over death in favor of a happier subject: resurrection. And that is something we must not do. We must confront the cross head-on and ask the difficult question: If death doesn't fix things—if it's *bad*—then what exactly happened on Golgotha?

Hints and Hushed Whispers

Not surprisingly, there are some hints within Scripture that tell us something about why Christ's execution is different from the others throughout human history. Hundreds of years before Jesus, a prophet named Isaiah wrote of a so-called Suffering Servant who would take upon himself the sins and hurts of God's people in order to bring about redemption.

The Servant would be "pierced for our transgressions"; he would be "crushed for our iniquities"; and his "punishment" would bring us peace. He would be cut off from the land of the living, and be assigned a grave with the wicked, though he had done no violence. But this would be no random, senseless death. According to Isaiah, the Servant's death would be a kind of sacrifice— an act of atonement for all the evil and violence that had seeped under the door into God's good world. It would be as if this Servant were actually taking all the ugliness onto himself so that the penalty for sin might be averted from God's people. It would be as if he were throwing himself on the grenade and absorbing the explosion (see Isaiah 53).

Yet this picture of Christ's death raises questions. For instance: How does the punishment of an innocent person fix anything for the guilty? How is that good news? To use a loose analogy, if I get busted for a serious crime, say, beating my wife or defrauding the elderly, how does it solve anything if Mother Teresa (or some other exemplary person) agrees to go to jail on my behalf? You might say that this *solution* sounds even worse than the crime itself.

So what qualifies Jesus to take the rap for us? Perhaps the beginning of an answer can be traced back to where this chapter began, with the idea of an author stepping into the artwork in order to relive the human drama in our place. Think of it like this: to change the course of any story, one needs not only a *writer* but a *character* as well. And as the God-man, Jesus fills both roles. Because sin is first and foremost a crime against God, it is only as God himself that Jesus can conquer and forgive it. Yet because death was a penalty for human sin (Adam's and our own), it is only as the true Adam (the representative of the entire human race) that Jesus can step into the void on our behalf.[5]

Christ may rightly bear our penalty because somehow all humanity is bound up *with* him through a mysterious connection. For this reason, Paul can even claim that he was "crucified *with* Christ" so that he no longer lives, but Christ lives in him (Gal. 2:20). To be united with Christ means that what happened to him has happened to us at some deep level—because we are joined together with him.

But what is the source of this mysterious connection? Perhaps it goes back to our origins. Because all humans were fashioned in Christ's "image" (Gen. 1:26), the Son is the rightful head of the entire human race. And in the Bible, the head often acts on the behalf of the whole. We see a picture of this reality in the way a king might stand in for his people—in their place—like David going out to meet Goliath on behalf of Israel. In modern terms, we see another loose analogy in the way the head of a company may willingly take the fall for a wrong done by a low-level employee. In the Bible, the people are bound up with their head. And for this reason, Christ may rightly pay the penalty for human evil—enduring even the ultimate exile (death) on our behalf. In so doing, he not only pays the price for sin, he also wins the victory as he conquers it. In so doing, he also sets the ultimate example of love that calls forth imitation.[6]

John's gospel paints a heart-wrenching portrait of this very truth. Toward the end of John's narrative, a bruised and bloodied Jesus is trotted out before a mob. He is clad only in a silly purple cloak and a thorny crown. They are mocking him. "Here's your poser-king!" is the intended jest. "Here's the fool who thought he could take the throne!" Yet even here, amid the mockery, Pilate's introduction of the dress-up king says it all. In the Latin language, his statement can be boiled down to just two words: *Ecce homo*. "Behold the man."[7]

He doesn't ask them to behold *a man*. He says, behold the man. Behold *the* human. And without knowing it, the Roman thug has identified Jesus for who he really is. He is the true representative of the entire human race. He is the true Adam whose actions will affect the world in an even more dramatic fashion. He is also the true Israel who will now fulfill the calling of the covenant. Behold *the* man. And behold the king! Like David his fore-father, Jesus is going to battle without armor, on behalf of the people, and their fate is bound up inextricably with his own. This is the fight we've been waiting for. It is the decisive battle to secure salvation for God's people. Behold the man![8]

In the searing image of a bloody king, we begin to glimpse the true meaning of the cross. There is love and logic there, if only in hints and hushed whispers. The cross is where God acted decisively to deal with the evil infecting his good creation. He acted. And he did so through the only vessel strong enough to bear the blow: his Son, the second Adam, the Author-Actor who did what only God could do and paid what only man could pay. Behold the man!

This is but one facet of the cross's meaning. It was the field of combat where an unlikely revolutionary— God in human flesh—secured the Creator's victory for all time. What happened there dwarfs our theories and defies our every attempt to distill its meaning. Yet if we believe the Scriptures, the crushing, freeing claim of the Bible is that one dark Friday, the Author of God's plotline allowed the cruelest twist of plot to waste itself on him. And because of this, the early followers of Jesus came to believe that in a very real sense, evil had been swallowed up in love. It is paradoxical that we could live forgiven because God died condemned. It is madness in a way. Yet as even Nietzsche knew: "There is always some madness in love. And there is always some reason in madness."[9]

The cross reminds us this is true. It tells us that our sin is serious. It is so ugly that God would have to die to make it beautiful. But the Jesus chapter doesn't end just yet.

Resurrection: Bootlegs and Black Dirt

I still have a weathered, old recording of a Rich Mullins concert. And somewhere in the middle of the concert, there is a point when Rich starts to tell a story about how his father passed away, of all places, in the family garden.

It's a sad story, and as Rich starts telling it you can hear the audience voice their sympathy (because, as you know now, *death is bad*). But in his odd way, Rich corrects the crowd for their lack of understanding. He says that when you get down to it, his father died rather well. He died well, Rich says, because the last thing he saw before meeting Jesus was the face of his lovely wife, pulling weeds beside him, and the cool black dirt of the garden he loved to tend.

I don't have a garden. But if I did, I don't think that's where I'd like to die. Still I do like the idea of having Brianna's face be the last thing I see. Because Brianna's face has always seemed radiant to me, and I figure it might lessen the shock of seeing heaven.

But they buried Jesus in a garden. And for the longest time that didn't seem the least bit interesting to me. Some years ago, though, I was reading another writer who made a very good point. He said that it makes sense for Jesus to reclaim life in a place like this, because creation starts *in a garden*. And if God really is putting the universe back together one atom at a time, then a garden would be a splendid touch of irony. In fact, it would almost make you think that God is a Storyteller at heart.[10]

Sir, Are You the Gardener?

So Jesus is resurrected, of all places, in a garden. And he appears first to a flustered woman named Mary. She's flustered because she has come to prepare his corpse for permanent burial. But now she sees it isn't there. Someone has heisted it away! She starts to weep. And so it is through salty tears that she sees Jesus and confuses him for the gardener.

Or does she?

I find it interesting that the resurrected Jesus doesn't correct Mary's words. He doesn't say, "No, actually, Mary, I'm *not* the gardener; my name is Jesus. Remember? We used to hang out!" He doesn't say that at all. Instead, he says her name: "Mary."

And she knows it's him.

When Jesus says her name, Mary realizes the truth behind the Gospels: the *Gardener* is Jesus, and he's alive. He's been resurrected. And a story this good starts to circulate faster than a rumor at a church picnic. Soon word spreads to the men (who, big surprise, do not believe the women). So Jesus appears to them too. And in all these instances the Savior does what only flesh and blood can do. He eats fish, he eats some bread, and he lets them touch him. He does what only humans can do, and then *he does some more*. You might say, he isn't less human than before; he's more human.[11] He passes through an unlocked door, he walks on water, and then, when you least expect it, he leaves.

And this leaving, as it often does, complicates things. It complicates matters because had the resurrected Jesus simply stuck around, it would be easy for us to measure his importance. If he had just stayed and cured cancer, wrote a self-help book, or invented a longer lasting light-bulb, *then* maybe we could all believe in him. (Maybe. It bears noting that not all believed the first time.) But he didn't stick around. He left. And this leaving leads us to the question with which the chapter began: What difference does this Jesus make?

The Difference: Meals Matter

I am more and more convinced that the best way to answer tough questions is to just start talking about food. Yes, food. Because in the Bible *eating* is important. In the Bible, meals matter. And nowhere is this truer than at the end of the Jesus-chapter.

In the beginning of God's Story, a man named Adam shares a meal with his wife, Eve, and according to the writer: "their eyes were opened." When this happened, it seemed that a distance also opened in Adam and Eve's most important relationships. A painful fissure opened in their relationship with God, with each other, and with the created order. Their eyes were opened, and for the first time, humanity saw the naked ugliness of broken community.

Ironically, another eye-opening experience takes place just after Jesus' resurrection. In a story from Luke's gospel, two of Jesus' friends—a man named Cleopas and a woman, probably his wife (hint, hint)—are walking down the road. It is three days after the bloody cruci-fixion. And as the husband and wife are walking, they speak about how they had hoped this revolutionary named Jesus would bring about the renewal of Israel. In other words, they had hoped he would pull a Guevara, overthrow the Romans, and take back the land.

But he didn't. Instead, he got himself nailed to a Roman cross, and as far as anybody in the first century was concerned, that was the end. A dead Messiah was a failed Messiah. End of story.

So the husband and wife are walking and sulking when they are joined quite suddenly by none other than Jesus himself. But they don't recognize him. (Apparently Jesus is disguising his identity like Brad Pitt in a Hollywood burger joint.) In other words, it's Jesus, but he's *incognito*. Upon joining the husband and wife, Incognito-Jesus asks them what they are talking about, and it's then that they start in with the long, sad story of wasted hopes on a would-be Messiah.

It's a false story, of course, and by the time they're finished we sense that Jesus has had just about enough. So with that he launches into what must have been the greatest sermon ever given (none of which is recorded by Luke, thank you very much!). Beginning with Moses and the Prophets, Jesus explains how *all* of the Old Testament has been a kind of movie trailer leading up to his arrival. He is the suffering Messiah who had to die in order to fulfill the Scriptures. The whole plotline has been pointing forward to him.

He says this, and they're captivated. Their hearts are burning inside them. Yet all the time they're wondering: *Who is this dude?* After a while, the couple convinces Incognito-Jesus to share a meal with them. And it's during this *meal* that the switch is finally flipped. As they take and eat the broken bread, Luke says: "Their eyes were opened" and they recognize the Savior (see Luke 24:13–35).

Two meals.

Two different parts of God's Story.

One result: *their eyes were opened.*

In the first meal, a man and woman eat, their eyes are opened, and creation splits apart at the seams. In the second meal, a man and woman eat, their eyes are opened, and they recognize the resurrected Jesus sitting there in front of them.

In the first meal, eyes are opened and this signals the severing of life's most meaningful relationships. In the second meal, eyes are opened and this signals, somehow, that *through Jesus* these relationships can be put back together.[12] Marriages, friendships, international feuds, issues of self-hatred, environmental atrocities—*all* may be made new. All may be set right. All may be healed, and there is no longer an excuse. Because of Jesus' resurrection, "More can be mended than you know."[13]

Because when God moves to rescue you before you think to ask him, something dangerous and compelling begins to happen inside of you. When God forgives your guilt through Jesus, you are freed up to do the same for others, even those who don't deserve it!

The incredible reality is that through Jesus, new creation has broken into our world. It bursts our corporate boxes and religious wineskins to announce, with bullhorn in hand, the end of our exile from God! Just as the old exodus started at a table with bread and wine, the new exodus starts with the same. It starts at a table with a non-violent revolutionary breaking bread with fair-weather friends and saying: "This is my body." Redemption is something to be tasted—not something to be dispassionately examined in the sterile confines of the intellect.

Renewed creation starts with a death-row Messiah gripping a sin-stained cup and proclaiming: "This is my blood, poured out for the forgiveness of the many" (see Matthew 26:26–29; Mark 14:22–26; Luke 22:14–20; and 1 Corinthians 11:24–25). And with this offer, we have the opportunity to retake our place at God's great table. With this offer, our eyes are opened, and we realize, trembling, *that no relationship is too far gone.* I'll say that again: no relationship is too far gone! We must give and forgive. We must join Jesus in walking out of exile, not because of guilt, but because of grace. Through his shattered body and spilled blood, we have been reunited with God. And it is now our life's calling to spread the revolution.

This is why Jesus matters! He matters because by coming and living and dying and rising again, he paved the way for the most unconventional uprising in human history. It is a revolution of love. By stepping onto the stage, he did what Adam and Abram and Israel could not. He accomplished the great mission of Israel to be a light to the world and the way back to true communion. He paved the way for new creation to come screaming back into the old.

The truth is this: because the Author donned the makeup of the actors, neither Romeo, nor Juliet, nor you or I must lay dead in the end. Because the Artist stepped into the artwork, the picture can be different. Because the Director set down the clipboard and walked into the screenplay, the plot can be forever mended.

Engage the Story

Having read about the Jesus-chapter in God's Story, it's time now to engage with it yourself. Read the following passages this week, reflect upon their meaning, and be prepared to discuss them with others:

- Luke 1:26–33; 2:1–20 (Jesus' birth)
- Matthew 3:13–7:29 (Baptism, temptation, and teachings)
- Mark 4:1–34 (Parables)
- John 4:46–6:59 (Miracles)
- Luke 22:14–24:53 (The climax of Jesus' earthly ministry)

Discuss the Story

1. Just when all seemed hopeless for Israel, a baby boy named Jesus was born in a forgotten corner of the Roman Empire.

   - Why was the birth of Jesus referred to as a royal birth and a royal scandal?
   - Why do you think the ruling authorities worked so hard to have the baby Jesus killed? What was so dangerous about this infant?

- Why do you think the violence and messiness of the original Christmas story get glossed over in favor of a sentimental greeting-card-style holiday?

2. Jesus led the life of a non-violent revolutionary. Yet this picture is often clouded by false images of Jesus, on the one hand, from the pop culture and, on the other hand, by some Christians. Discuss the following statement with this in mind.

On the one hand, pop culture has led us to think of grown-up Jesus as a kind of a first-century Oprah. He was a compassionate if somewhat effeminate man who delivered good advice and tried to help people. According to the portraits, he likely spent most of his time cuddling baby lambs and offering a gospel of warm fuzzies to a world with low self-esteem.

On the opposite extreme, we've been led by some in the church to think of Jesus' life in purely spiritual terms. He was, from this perspective, a kind of benevolent ticket scalper, handing out free passes to the afterlife. For this Jesus, the goal was simple: he came to earth so we could leave it. Thus, the churchy-Jesus usually asks us just one question: Do you want to go to heaven when you die?

- One problem with churchy-Jesus is the fact that the Jesus of Scripture spends much of his time talking about what it would look like for the kingdom of God to come "on earth" (Luke 11:2), not somewhere up in heaven. Have you ever thought about Jesus' message in this way? Why might we ignore this aspect of Christ's message?

3. The Scriptures also seem to make clear that Jesus was not only a non-violent revolutionary, but also *God in the flesh*.

   - What does it tell us about the depth of our predicament that the Author of the Story would have to step into the narrative to rescue the plot from sure disaster?
   - Read Philippians 2:1–8 and discuss it together.

4. When Jesus died a traitor's death on a Roman cross, his followers were both shocked and confused. Their basic assumption was the same as ours: death is bad. Death means your would-be Messiah was a failure.

   - Read Isaiah 53:3–5, 10–12 together. How does this passage shed light on the reason why Jesus had to die on behalf of God's people?
   - Reflect on this statement as a group.

     Because sin is first and foremost a crime against God, it is only as God himself that Jesus can forgive it. And because death is first and foremost a punishment for human wickedness (Adam's and our own), it is only as a kind of Second Adam (the ultimate human representative) that Jesus can step into the void on our behalf. It is only as the true representative of the entire human community that Jesus can pay the penalty for human evil. And it is only as the true representative of God himself that his sacrifice can be successful.

   - How does Pilate's scornful phrase "Behold the man" sum up Jesus' mission and identity?

5. Three days after Jesus' bloody death, God raised him
    back to life.

    •   Why is it important that Jesus would be resur-
        rected in a garden?
    •   Mary believed in Christ's resurrection when Jesus
        said her name. Reflect on what it was that led you
        to believe in Jesus' resurrection. If you are not
        at a point of belief yet, talk about what makes
        believing in the resurrection difficult for you.
    •   How does the resurrection prove or *vindicate*
        Jesus' message during his ministry?

6. Read the story in Luke 24:13–31.

    •   How does the meal in this passage tie together
        with the story of Adam and Eve? What does this
        tell us about how God is using Jesus to put the
        world back together?
    •   Spend some time, as a group or individually,
        asking God to open your eyes to the truth about
        who Jesus was, and what he did for all of us. Think
        about this passage the next time you receive
        communion.
    •   Reflect on the following words in closing:

    We must give and forgive. We must join Jesus in
    walking out of exile, not because of guilt, but because
    of grace. Through the shattered body and spilled
    blood, we have been reunited with God. And it is now
    our life's calling to spread the revolution.

CHURCH

Why You Shouldn't Buy My Business Book

I've decided that my next big writing project will be to craft one of those *uber* trendy business books like the kind I've seen for sale in airports. You know the ones. As far as I can tell, they are usually brightly colored with a bizarre title that is designed to get your attention by making you think: *That's absurd! I must read more.*

In saying this, I should probably admit that I *ought* to have no business writing a book on business. I can't balance a checkbook and (come to think of it) I don't even know where mine is at the moment. Yet having looked over some of the successful titles in the genre, I am increasingly convinced that such knowledge is in no way a prerequisite. So I'm going to write a biz book, and I've even got some ideas for what it will be about.

The first idea details the innovative research techniques I employed to start a successful multinational shoe company from a stall inside a Starbucks bathroom. It will be groundbreaking. And because I assume the book will pretty much write itself, I've spent most of my time working on a snappy title. (Because let's be honest, that's the most important part.) I'm thinking something edgy but poignant, like: *Rid'n Shot-Gun: Insights on Shoes and Business from the Next Stall Over*. Look for it in airports soon.

My other idea is subtler (if that's possible). It deals with something folks in the business world call "buzz marketing." In truth, I haven't the foggiest idea what buzz marketing is, but I don't see that as a major problem. The book will detail the time-tested insights I gained from selling crashed-out mail-order NASCARS to Amish farm girls from Pennsylvania. I'm calling it: *Unleash Your Inner Horsepower!—Secrets to Success for the Pre-Industrial, Post-Feminist Pit-Crew*. My lawyers are working out the repercussions.

By this point, you're probably wondering what motivated me to write on such topics. To be honest, I became enamored with such *uber* trendy biz books from working in a local church. While I am a professor now, I began my life after school by pastoring in a local church plant. It was a fantastic experience. Yet the more time I began to spend with up-and-coming ministers, the more I was informed that apparently *these* were the kind of books that I was supposed to be reading. And on one level, it makes sense. After all, there are many insights that pastors should learn from the world of corporate CEOs and free-market competition. There's some wisdom to be garnered from the realm of business. But after a while, this constant focus on the world of commerce and commodity began to raise some questions.

In one instance, I bumped into a good friend (also a pastor) who told me he was reading the latest best seller on time management. (We'll leave aside whether that last sentence is an oxymoron. Let's be charitable and say it isn't.) The book's title was *The Four-Hour Work Week*. I didn't ask about the subtitle. I figured it was something straightforward, like *How to Get Fired . . . by Tuesday*. It was after this conversation that I decided to cash in on the apparently burgeoning market for pastors-buying-business-books-by-people-with-no-business-writing-business-books. It's a specific niche, but I figure I'm as qualified as anyone.

Unfortunately, as I began to scour the Scriptures for material to put in my upcoming publication, I faced a disheartening realization. After reading all 976 pages of my leather-bound NIV, I was astonished to find nary a single mention of the Holy Three (buzz marketing, power lunches, and mail-order NASCARS), though I'm hoping further knowledge of rabbinic literature will yield some new results.

Corpus Christi

What I found in the Scriptures was something different. I found that when the Bible speaks about the church, it speaks *not* of a business—with CEOs, marketing gurus, and white-toothed motivational speakers—but of a body, with arms and eyes and elbows. And this seems strange. It seems odd, because while we think of many things when someone says church—a building with a steeple, the place I decided to trust Jesus, a negative experience with flannel-graph and songs with actions—one thing we typically do not think of is a human physique, complete with all the requisite appendages. People have bodies, we say; churches have building programs. There's a difference.

Yet as we look back in time, we see that this distinction has not always been in place. The Latin-speaking Christians even had a name for their body-church. They called it *corpus Christi*. And while this may now bring to mind a sweaty town in South Texas, to older Christians the words meant something very different. They referred, in a very real sense, to the very "body of Christ" that now exists on earth: *corpus Christi*.[1]

This chapter is about that body. It's about the church. For as we've seen, that is the next installment in the long Story of the Bible: creation, fall, Israel, Jesus, church. But at its core, the chapter is an attempt to answer a simple question: What does it mean to *be* the body of Jesus here on planet Earth? What does it mean to be a *body* at a time when some churches look an awful lot like businesses; and when some pastors read more on buzz marketing than they do the Bible? What does it mean to be a corpus that is more than just a corporation?

To answer that last question, we need to leave the world of biz books and arrive at a Middle Eastern hilltop where, at the moment, a bunch of young men stand dumbstruck and looking at the sky.

Liftoff

According to the Bible, it was at a place like this that the resurrected Jesus uttered a few spare words to his friends before ascending to the heavens. Granted, the word "ascending" isn't one we use as much these days (except in reference to elevators or airplanes). In this case, that's because it involves a kind of street-magician levitation that most of us do not possess. Hence the thought of Jesus ascending can be a bit strange. Yet for me, it has never been the most difficult part of this passage. In my mind, the most difficult portion of the text involved what Jesus *said* before he floated upward. According to one writer, he looked his friends in the eyes and told them that he would be with them *always* (see Matthew 28:20).

It's a simple promise really. Jesus says that he will be with his disciples forever. Then it gets complicated. Because just after saying this, the Savior promptly turns and breaks his promise. Or so it seems. Think about that for a moment. The Gospels end with Jesus saying to his friends, "I'll be with you always. I will *never* leave you." And then he leaves. And for many of the confused folks on the hillside, this is the last time (this side of heaven) that they see Jesus.

It's a disconcerting story, especially for those of us who have been abandoned by someone. When I was young, I had a friend whose dad said something just like this. He said that he would still be around after the divorce. He said he'd always be there to play catch and go fishing. But then he wasn't. Instead he found a new wife and a new family and he just sort-of ascended right out of the old one. He broke his promise, and while I'm no psychologist, I can't imagine that's an easy thing to handle. It's a contradiction. And the contradiction makes the leaving that much harder. Did Jesus do that?

The Gospel and Celine Dion

Christ's parting words *ought* to make us scratch our heads at first. If they don't, it may be because we've spent so much time in the Christian subculture that we have developed an uncanny ability to gloss over any apparent oddities within the Bible. This may sound like a virtue, but I don't think it is. I think it can be a subtle way of ignoring God's Word.

On the other hand, perhaps our lack of consternation over Jesus' strange good-bye stems from another source. Perhaps it stems from the way in which we've learned to speak of his continued presence in terms that are vaguely reminiscent of a cheesy ending to a cheesy movie. "He may be gone," we say, "but he lives forever in our hearts." We invited him in there one time at a youth camp, and that's where he lives now. We say this often enough and somewhere in the background I hear Celine Dion start singing the theme song from *Titanic*.

Because if the Bible were a movie, the ascension would be a natural time to roll the credits and cut to a greeting-card commercial. It would sell lots of greeting cards. It's a heart-wrenching moment. And the metaphor of Jesus living on in our hearts carries a certain senti-mental ring to it, like when Leo and Kate let go amid the ice floe. Yet, in the end, this kind of talk rings somewhat hollow. It rings hollow because to speak of Jesus in this way is to speak of him just as we do a deceased relative or a long-lost love. "They'll be with us forever," we say, "in our hearts." And we don't really mean it, of course. We just mean that we'll remember them forever, and that their absence is still deeply felt.

Unfortunately, when it comes to Jesus, this heartfelt metaphor is not enough. Christ does not literally live in our hearts. We know this. And if we don't, we can seek clarification from our cardiologist. It's an expression. Yet it does raise some interesting implications about the strange promise on the hilltop.

Jesus' final good-bye seems to force us into a decision. Either Jesus is *with us* only in our sentimental memories (like Aunt Edna, or that long-lost love), or he is a deceiver who simply lied and left. Either Jesus was speaking very metaphorically about remaining with us, or he is an untruthful phony and the spiritual equivalent of a deadbeat dad. After all, you cannot tell your friends that you'll be joining them for dinner only to grab your coat and leave before the appetizer. So here's the question: Why did the early Christians begin to speak of the Lord quite seriously as though he were *with them*? The answer brings us to the day of Pentecost.

Like Oxygen

One of the most astonishing turns in God's drama involves the way in which early Christians came to believe that Jesus really was *with* and *in* them, in a way beyond mere sentiment. They believed this so strongly, in fact, that when it came time to mark the birth of God's expanded family (the church), the early disciples looked to a moment *after* the ascension.

It was a day called Pentecost, and the disciples pointed to it as the time when the Breath of Jesus blew into the lives and lungs of ordinary people, like oxygen into empty chests.

According to the early Jesus-followers, the church's chapter began at the moment when God exhaled his Spirit from the resurrected body of Jesus into the sin-scarred bodies of his people. Folks like you and me. It was a kind of divine CPR, and the effects were tangible. People were changed. They said it was this Breath, or Spirit, that enabled broken individuals—racists, cowards, and thieves—to begin to speak and live in ways that actually made the world a more beautiful place. They began to speak and live in ways that conformed to a Jesus-style way of being.

It was God's Spirit that allowed ordinary people to do what Adam and Abram could not; it empowered them to be part of God's final work, the work of restoring the world and ushering true community back into shattered creation.

The Old Testament prophet Ezekiel spoke of something like this. Hundreds of years before Jesus, Ezekiel had a vision of a valley littered with parched and sun-bleached bones. They were the bones of God's people, dead and decomposed. Then Ezekiel heard this:

> "This is what the Sovereign LORD says to these
> bones: I will make *breath* enter you, and you will

come to life. I will attach tendons to you and make flesh come upon you and cover you with skin; I will put *breath* in you, and you will come to life. Then you will know that I am the LORD." (Ezek. 37:5–6, emphasis mine)

Just as it did in Genesis, God's Breath (Spirit) breathes life into barrenness. But that's not all. The most fascinating part of Ezekiel's vision involves *what* the Spirit forms out of the dry and scattered bones. It does not form a corporation, a denomination, or a civic club—it forms a *corpus*. In Ezekiel's vision, God's Breath forms bodies with tendons, flesh, and life. It's a spiritual equation: Breath → Body.

When early Christians began to reread Ezekiel, we can only imagine that they thought of Pentecost. It was on this day, while Jesus' followers were gathered in Jerusalem, that God's Spirit-wind blew in and changed their lives forever. It was as if the disciples breathed it in and were empowered to become the kind of people— the kind of *body*—that could take the Jesus-message to the ends of the earth.

God's Breath was God's presence. And the presence of Jesus compelled Christians to feel neither abandoned, nor comforted in a shallow sentimental sense. The Breath of Pentecost caused people to believe that God really was inside them. His *Breath* was with them, giving them new life and new vitality. And in this moment, the church was born.

Yet the day was about more than just Wind; there was also fire and tongues. And such things demand some explanation too.

Fire-Tongues and Four-Letter Words

After the rushing "wind" of Acts 2, we learn that
tiny flames also appeared above the heads of Christ's
followers. This was a signal that God's presence now
dwelt inside them, just as it had within the temple.[2]
Their bodies became, in essence, movable temples, made
sacred by Christ's blood and Breath. But there were
more than just little tongues of flame above their heads.
There were also tongues of another sort—that is, miraculous *languages* that they now began to speak, so as to
proclaim the gospel message.

These early Christians spoke in tongues. And when
I think about this fiery language, I also think about a
friend of mine named Sully (not his real name). Sully does
stand-up comedy at a local nightclub called "Dr. Grins."
We met because a good friend of mine—we'll call him
Pastor Chad (absolutely his real name)—decided he
would try his hand at a new profession: stand-up comedy.
It seems he heard about an upcoming open-mic night at
the club and thought to himself: *What could be funnier
than a straight-laced evangelical trying to pull laughs from
a bunch of half-blitzed party people?* Turns out, not much.

So I tagged along one night with my pastor to the
nightclub, and it was there that he introduced me to
Sully. In many ways, they couldn't be more different. Yet
it was obvious that the two had struck up a friendship.

As he would be quick to tell you, Sully was not a
Christian. So you can imagine my surprise when Pastor
Chad told me he had invited his new friend to do stand-up
at an upcoming event for local pastors! It had been

labeled as a "Pastor Appreciation Dinner," and Sully was to be part of the entertainment. I thought perhaps it was a kind of payback for all those pagans who decided to invite the Christians to the Coliseum to entertain them.

So naturally, I tagged along.

We rode to the event together in the pastoral minivan, and on the way, we discussed what jokes were and were not appropriate. Most of Sully's material landed firmly in the "not appropriate" category, but in the end, he assured us that he could sterilize a list that would pass Jerry Falwell's all-points inspection.

And surprisingly, it worked.

For the first fifteen seconds of Sully's act, not a single sketchy reference slipped through. Then all hell broke loose. As I looked up at the stage I could see him perspiring heavily as he looked out on a room that was practically brimming with non-alcoholic beverages. I could read his mind: *Why did I say yes to this?*

Then somewhere amid the nervousness, in this room of very conservative preachers and their wives, a *word* slipped out. And then another. It was happening in slow motion. And as it happened, I could hear the air being sucked out of the room. This was going to end badly! I started preparing to warm up the pastoral minivan. Unfortunately, it wasn't over.

Further into his routine, Sully got more nervous and a couple more words slipped out, along with some jokes that were hardly clean by Christian standards. People weren't laughing now. Not even a little bit. And Sully didn't look so good. After all, these were his tame jokes! They always worked. They always got laughs! But not tonight. And at some point, toward the end, it was as if he said "forget it—I'm going with my usual routine!" They cut his mic.

Afterward, most folks were surprisingly polite. One lady even tried to pay Sully a compliment by telling him that when she was an "unbeliever" she would never have had the courage to come to an event like this. Sully didn't think of himself as an unbeliever. He believed in lots of things, just not basic Christian doctrines. He was offended, and he asked about it later: "What the [bleep] is an unbeliever?!"

Later, as Brianna and I drove home, we alternated between fits of nervous laughter and feelings of embarrassment. I hate watching people bomb. Because I've bombed. And it stinks. Then as I lay awake in bed, I thought strangely about something that happened at Pentecost with the fiery tongues.

The Scriptures say that when Jesus' Breath blew into the lives of his followers, a crowd of people gathered to see what had happened. And it wasn't just a crowd of locals. They were Jews from various different countries and languages, all gathered for the feast. Yet they had come together now because they had heard the disciples speaking to them in their own language (see Acts 2:6).

The Bible calls this cross-cultural communication "speaking in tongues," but I imagine it was something different from the apparently self-induced hysterics of some Christian cable shows. In Acts 2, these tongues appear to be real (human) languages with real words. They were native languages that made sense to the people gathered from their far-flung lands. They made so much sense, in fact, that the people wondered how a bunch of backwater-types from Galilee could communicate the Jesus-story so clearly. It was a miracle, and after my night at the R-rated pastor's dinner, it seemed like an even bigger one.[3]

Why I Want to Speak in Tongues

For many of us, it isn't long after being converted that we lose much of our ability to communicate the Jesus-story to people like Sully. We no longer speak the same language. And before long, we just stop hanging out with those who aren't like us. That's the way it often goes, and it's tragic, because somewhere along the line even our compliments start to sound offensive. We start to say things like: "You're pretty brave, for an *un*believer."

And folks like Sully have just as much trouble communicating with us. They don't know our rules. What is acceptable? What is offensive? And if they do, the rules seem arbitrary. I know that Sully felt this way because somewhere in the middle of a blog post about the debacle at the pastors' dinner, he asked why it was okay for evangelicals to make fun of Catholics (one of the biggest laughs of the night had been a fairly innocuous Catholic joke), but for some reason, saying a four-letter word for "poop" could get you in big, big trouble. After all, he thought, aren't Catholics *people*? And isn't poop just *poop*?

He didn't get it. And for many of the pastors, the feeling was mutual. Around the room with our dinner rolls and our sensible shoes, many of us looked a lot alike. We looked like Sully. Most of us were middle-class Americans with mortgages, kids in braces, and a weakness for fried food. But despite the similarities, we spoke a different language. It involved many of the same vowels and consonants, but it was different nonetheless. It was different enough that most of us had about as much chance of communicating the gospel meaningfully to Sully, as we had communicating it meaningfully to a golden retriever. It wasn't going to happen, and that night it hit me.

So for the first time in my Christian existence, I prayed that God would allow me to speak in tongues. Not exactly like the big-haired TV preachers. But in a way analogous to how they did at Pentecost. I prayed that Jesus would breathe his Breath into me and grant me the ability to communicate his story in ways that make sense to Cretans, Arabs, and stand-up comedians. I prayed for a language that outsiders could understand. And even as I prayed this, I had to admit that if it does happen, it will be a miracle.

But then again, I believe in those.

Step Two Must Die

Unfortunately, for all of its importance, the day of Pentecost lasts only twenty-four hours. It comes like a flash flood in Acts 2, and it's over by chapter 3. It is one day, and although it alters human history forever, it is barely a blip on the chronological radar. The fire-tongues and Spirit-Breath are impressive, but after the emotion of the church's birthday subsides, the baby needs to grow up. And if my seventh-grade yearbook picture is any indication, growing up involves some awkwardness in the transition.

For the early church, the primary growing pain involved a difficult question: Would Christianity be open to all cultures and ethnicities, or would it remain the private property of a select few? Would the Jesus-revolution remain a race-and-tribe-based club, or would it grow into the fulfillment of God's promise to Abraham that all nations would be blessed?

The question arose because the earliest disciples were members of a single cultural and religious heritage. They were Jewish. And they did Jewish things. They worshipped at the Jewish temple, ate Jewish (kosher) food, and read extensively from the Jewish Scriptures. They were children of Abraham, and in this sense, their faith was a family thing. In the minds of some folks (called the Judaizers), you could join the family, but that required a two-step process.

Step #1: Leave your old allegiances (to money, power, idolatry) and place your faith in Jesus.

Step #2: For Gentiles, leave your cultural heritage (the ethnic identity you were raised with) and become a Jew.

Both steps were difficult. The first step was hard because it involved acknowledging the authority of a new Ruler (or Lord) at a time when many false gods (including Caesar) demanded one's worship and allegiance. The second was difficult because it involved rejecting one's heritage, one's culture, and in essence, one's identity. And if this were not enough, for adult males, step two meant going under the knife for an operation that would make even a linebacker cry like a baby: circumcision.[4]

It was step two that was keeping non-Jews out of the Jesus-movement, and for good reason. The shame of publicly renouncing one's ethnic and cultural heritage brings to mind some of the worst chapters in human history: genocide, lynch-mobs, ethnic cleansing. It brings to mind the old photographs of Native Americans forced to cut their hair and put on choking neckties in order to be *Christianized*—by which was meant: be made white. Such ethnocentrism dredges up the memories of African slaves who were caught and shipped like cargo to a foreign land where they would be given *Christian names* for life in a *Christian country*.

We may cringe at such practices today, but the church's biggest conflict after Pentecost revolved around this question: Should following the God of Jesus (the God of Abraham, Isaac, and Jacob) require the rejection of one's original ethnic identity? Did it require a person to *become Jewish*, by virtue of the law of Moses, in order to become a Christian? In other words: What should be done with step two?

What the early Jesus-followers did with the so-called second step is truly astonishing. In the face of numerous Old Testament rules on everything from circumcision, meat, and table fellowship, the young leaders of the church eventually reached a startling conclusion: *step two must die.*

The requirement that Gentiles must adhere fully to the Jewish law had to be rubbed out in the hearts and minds of Jesus-followers. It had to die. And with it, dozens of scriptural laws that were meant only for the Israel chapter would be set aside, not because they were bad, but because they had been fulfilled in Christ.

If this sounds like blasphemy to you, then you know precisely how some early Christians felt. Tough questions arose within the church: Are not those commands on circumcision and food laws still in the Bible? Isn't Scripture God's *unchanging* Word? What gives us the right to ignore some laws—the ones against eating pork, or getting your penis snipped—while still holding on to other laws: like the ones on murder and monotheism? Their answer went something like this: while God never changes, certain commands belong to certain chapters in his plotline.[5] Thus, strange as it sounds: *God doesn't want us to do everything the Bible says.*

Why You Shouldn't Do Everything the Bible Says

If that statement disconcerts you, let me clarify: you shouldn't obey *all* the commands in Scripture, not because the Liberal-progressive-revisionists-who-probably-live-in-California say so, but because the Bible does.

In our chapter on Israel, we made the case that Yahweh handed down some laws for a rather subversive reason. He gave them to preserve his people culturally even as they refused to stand out morally. As the Old Testament makes clear, Israel's hearts were no better than those of the nations. All humans stand enslaved to sin. Therefore, it was because God's children were no different on the inside (with regard to their hard hearts) that God preserved them by making them different on the outside. This is one reason for the proliferation of religious rules on everything from pork to penises.

But surface differences (on everything from food to fabrics) were never the Creator's ultimate desire. God's desire was that Israel would stand out because of her love and fidelity to him. She was to care for the widow, the orphan, and the fatherless. She was to worship God alone, because all other gods will leave you high and dry, and Yahweh alone is worthy. In other words, God wanted Israel to express love for him through well-ordered love for others. That's it. This has always been God's one desire, in every phase of human history. Yet all of us have failed. Like *all* of us, Israel went her own way, she did what she thought best, and she became part of the problem rather than a part of the solution.

So (as we have seen) the Creator made a brilliant and surprising move. If Israel would be no different from the neighbors morally, then God would make her different culturally. And by this creative twist, God would sustain his family until *Someone* came along and lived out the *heart* of the commandments right down to the last punctuation mark.

Quite simply, Jesus filled that role. His life kept the soul of the Torah (the ancient law of Moses), his death paid the debt of sin, his resurrection proved his victory, and his bodily ascension made space for a new body here on earth—the church—his *corpus* filled with his Spirit.

Now, by grace alone, it is our job to continue the work of renewing creation through the same Spirit that hovered over the chaotic waters back in Genesis 1.

This is why some of the Old Testament laws on everything from circumcision to animal sacrifice no longer apply, *not* because they were bad, but because they belong specifically to another chapter in God's Story. They are like grand sailing ships once used to carry travelers from England to America. They were essential for the journey, but unnecessary upon the newfound land. Their good purpose was fulfilled. Because of Christ and his Spirit, we have reached the shoreline of a new reality. And on this shoreline, even grand old ships must be set aside. Not because they are bad, but because if we choose to stay aboard them, we will never experience life in God's new world.[6]

The old laws designed to set God's people apart on an ethnic and cultural level—and those sacrificial laws fulfilled by Jesus' work on the cross—have had their purpose satisfied. Hence, we live now in a new chapter. In this chapter, God's family is defined by a simpler quality. We are set apart, not by a nation, tribe, or common diet, but by our unflinching trust in Jesus Christ, and by our Spirit-driven growth in an obedience that is fueled by grace alone.

In this way, the story of the church is the story of ordinary people learning how to move inland, toward the mountains of God's new creation, from a sandy shoreline that was reached only by the work of Christ. And we see this truth most clearly in the letters of a fiery tentmaker named Paul.

What Paul Knew

With a reputation as a violent Jewish fundamentalist (Pharisee), Paul would seem an unlikely candidate for a loving outreach to the nations. Yet, in an instant, the one-time persecutor of Christians found himself *confronted* by the resurrected Jesus, *converted* to the Jesus-movement, and *convinced* that God's new chapter must involve an open invitation for even Gentiles to join the Jesus revolution without adopting all the Jewish boundary markers from the Old Testament.

Despised for this new stance, Paul faced opposition on all sides—from Jewish Christians (called Judaizers) who demanded a return to the good ole days of circumcision and food laws, and from a pagan empire bent on the politics of idolatry and exploitation. Both sides sought to silence Paul. Yet Paul faced both with the mind of a scholar, the heart of a pastor, and the grit of a ditch-digger. He was tough. But the years had taught him how to love. Because of this, Paul's writings leave us a detailed (if dense) blueprint for how we must approach the spiritual, political, and social questions of our own day.

More than anything, Paul knew that because of Jesus (and his Spirit inside us), Christians are to look at their neighbors and the world *not* in the divisive terms of the way it's always been, but in the hope-filled anticipation that God is moving even now to renew our broken world. We have reason to hope, because if God declared us right with him by grace and faith alone (Paul's term for this is *justification*), then no person is ever beyond hope. We live now with this conviction, and it drives us to do exactly what the tentmaker did after his encounter with the risen Jesus: bring this good news to the world.

In addition to a rejection of ethnocentric religion, Paul calls us to also subvert the pagan empires of our own day—the specters of money, sex, and political idolatry—with the message of a king named Jesus. And at the same time, he calls us to reject the false claims of a narrow religious legalism that seeks to convert people to Jesus *plus* some human list of rules that have no basis in the New Testament. We learn many things from Paul, but these two lessons are among the most important. We are to confront the idolatry of political regimes that demand what only God should have (ultimate allegiance) and a religious backwardness that would place race or rules above the grace of Jesus Christ. In such ways, Paul shows that God can guide us by the script of Scripture toward the final destination of his new creation.

This was Paul's conviction. And it's with this in mind that we turn to the question that started this chapter: What does it mean to be the body of Jesus here and now? Ironically, the answer may come (as it often did with Jesus) through a kind of parable.

Stratford's Honky-Tonk

Tucked away in the English countryside there sits a quaint old town called Stratford. The town itself is nestled in the woods of Warwickshire along a river called Avon. Yet Stratford is identified most commonly not by geographic location, but by the reputation of her most famous son, a tousle-headed playwright named Will.

And not far from Will's hometown, on what was once the winding road that led toward London, imagine that there sits today the well-worn stonework of what used to be a roadside inn.[7] It was, in its heyday, a kind of sixteenth-century honky-tonk (or pub) for tired travelers going to and from the city. The name is not important. What matters, according to locals, is that the establishment was famous for brewing the best ale in all of Warwickshire. But that was then. Today, some moss-covered stones are all that remain of the original structure. It was renovated several times through the centuries, rebuilt, and purchased by a widower, a retiring banker from nearby London.

His name is not important either. The important thing is what this banker *found* inside the sealed-off cellar of the roadside inn. There, inside a musty wooden chest, were the tattered remains of a yellowed manuscript—partly destroyed but mostly intact. And on its crinkled surface were the scrawling quill marks of an almost unreadable *olde* English. The banker almost threw it out. But in the end, it was his curiosity that caused him to ask questions.

In time, the manuscript made its way to London where grumpy men with thick glasses poured over its swirling letters. Tiny fragments were clipped off and tested. Then, nearly a month after almost trashing the contents of the chest, an extraordinary conclusion was relayed to the gray-haired London banker. The crinkled parchment was in fact a play, an as-yet undiscovered play, and one that bore all marks of Stratford's favorite son. It was the handiwork of William Shakespeare!

The banker almost fainted when they told him. In no time, scholars and camera crews arrived by London's Heathrow Airport to examine the long-lost play, and to discuss in different accents the importance of its rediscovery. It was, by all accounts, an extraordinary find—perhaps the most extraordinary of the century. But there was a massive problem. After an initial reading, it was clear that although the manuscript was quite extensive, the final act was missing.

As one neared the conclusion of the play, the crinkled parchment simply crumbled into dust. And with it, the play's climactic ending disappeared. Shakespeare's long-lost masterpiece would remain unfinished. Or so it seemed.

Channeling Shakespeare

Few know it, but it was the gray-haired banker who first voiced what seemed to be a risky proposition. "Suppose the end should *not* be lost forever?" he asked. "After all, a play is meant to be performed."

And with that, a plan unfolded that would allow the script to finally reach the stage. The concept was simple. The very best Shakespearian actors would be gathered from around the globe; they would be given guidance from scholars and directors; and by this guidance they would skillfully perform the parts that survived the cellar. Then came the twist. Because no great play should go unfinished, it was decided that the actors would immerse themselves in the plot of Shakespeare's drama. Then, as the fateful moment neared, the actors would simply *keep acting* through a kind-of faithful but creative improvisation.

Admittedly, it was a risky move. Almost everyone agreed that the previous acts belonged to Shakespeare. But the final act would remain, in part, a matter of careful and creative interpretation. Out of reverence for the original, no definitive ending would be tacked on by modern hands. Because to do so would assume a knowledge and power that only Shakespeare, the creator, could possess.

The final act would involve a kind of sacred improv, but of a kind that took into studied account the infallible content of the previous acts. These acts would set the course, and the actors would allow that script to guide their movements. The show would go on; and its authenticity would be measured by the degree to which the improvisation fit together with the author's preceding actions. Months of practice came and went, and finally it was time to raise the curtain.

Tension filled the theatre. And as often happens with courageous works of art, reviews were mixed. On some nights, the agreement was that the actors somehow veered off course, channeling influences other than Shakespeare. Some wanted bigger parts for themselves. And some failed merely out of ignorance and human fallibility. On some nights, the players lost the plot and the audience could tell, even if they had never read the script themselves.

But there were magical nights as well. On these evenings, the audience sat rapt as the actors seemed to channel the very soul of Shakespeare. It was poetry in motion, and even the unfinished act bore the bard's undeniable fingerprints. The performance was captivating, and on these nights, the crowd was heard to comment that it seemed the very spirit of the author was guiding every step and syllable.

On these nights, the actors' words and actions seemed indistinguishable from those of the writer. And on these nights, the gray-haired banker would stand in the wings with a wry smile. From there he would watch as even the worst of cynics came in with questions and left with wonder.

If you have ears to hear, then do so.

Learning to Act

To discover God's grand Story in the Bible is to discover a masterpiece unfinished. We have in books like Genesis, Numbers, and John, the previous movements—and we have also some hints as to the ending. Yet somewhere before the final curtain, the page breaks off.

The New Testament ends with a baby church stumbling forward into God's new world. And as this script crumbles away, we are left looking about us like dumbstruck disciples on that Middle Eastern hilltop. The Story breaks off, yet we're still here. And we face a choice.

On the one hand, we can simply repeat the earlier parts of the play verbatim (we might call this the fundamentalist option). On the other hand, we can ignore the earlier chapters as false, dead, or oppressive (we might call this the Liberal option). Or we can choose a more daring and faithful path. We can do with the Scriptures what was meant to be done with every drama. We can act! We can act in faithful but creative improvisation. We can immerse ourselves in the prior scenes: the Old and New Testaments. We can study, pray, and learn from these chapters in God's plotline. And then we can do something extraordinary. We can live, creatively and faithfully where we are—in the context of the new covenant. With God's Spirit moving us along, we can obey the call of Christ and Scripture. We can observe where the plot is going, learn from where it's been, and step into the drama.[8]

Like all actors, our performance will be judged. And as with every work of art, reviews may be mixed. Some days we will perform well, some days quite poorly. Some actors will make the story more credible by their grace-filled movements. Others will have the opposite effect. Some actors will be faithful but be judged as failures. (Remember Jesus?) And some will make the greatest drama ever written look like a low-budget B-rated disaster. (Remember the religious leaders?)

Yet, in the end, none of us can escape the reality that history is God's drama, the Scriptures are our script, and each of us must act. This is what it means to be a *corpus;* it's what it means to be Christ's body here on earth. To be an actor is to use a *body* to tell a better story. This is part of what it means to be the church.

It is the church's calling to tell God's Story with our lives and with our bodies. We do so in reference to the Scriptures because it is in the telling that the audience is invited into the drama. Yet as we go about our lives of work and worship, we do so knowing that the Author (not the crowd) will have the final word on our performance. His review is the only one that matters, and one day he will judge us all. But that's a subject for the next chapter.

Engage the Story

Having read about the church in God's Story, it's time now to engage with it yourself. Read the following passages this week, reflect upon their meaning, and be prepared to discuss them with others:

- Acts 2 (Pentecost)
- Acts 10 (A Gentile Pentecost)
- Romans 5–6; Hebrews 11 (Salvation by grace, through faith)
- Galatians 5:16–6:11; 1 John 2:28–3:24 (Living by the Spirit)

Discuss the Story

1. One of the most astonishing twists in God's drama involves the way in which the early Christians came to believe that Jesus really was *with them* in all that they were doing.

   - What event led to this belief that Jesus was working in and through the first Christians after the ascension?
   - Discuss the following statement:

   According to the early Jesus-followers, the church's chapter began at the moment when God exhaled his Spirit from the resurrected body of Jesus into the sin-scarred bodies of people like you and me. It was a kind of divine CPR, and the effects were tangible. People were changed; they said it was this Breath (God's oxygen inside them) that enabled broken individuals—racists, cowards, and thieves— to begin to speak and live in ways that actually made the world a more beautiful place.

- In what ways have you experienced the Holy Spirit transforming your heart and mind throughout your life? Be specific.

2. Read Acts 2:1–11 and then discuss the following questions:

- When God's Spirit came, the disciples suddenly found themselves communicating the Jesus-message meaningfully with people who were very different from them. Discuss a time when you were able to communicate the Jesus-message to someone who normally would not be receptive to it. When did someone do this for you?
- The writer makes the point that, in many cases, as we spend more time within the Christian subculture, we lose our ability to speak meaningfully (in a language that can be understood) to individuals outside the church. Why do you think this is? Have you seen it in your own life? How might it be avoided?
- It could be argued that one of the few universal languages is the language of compassion. The

early Christians spoke this language regularly through acts of love and service to the marginalized. How might you and your group begin to speak the universal language of compassion to those who need it most?

3. For the early church, the primary growing pain involved a difficult question: Would Christianity be open to all comers or would it remain the private property of a select few? Would the Jesus revolution remain a race-and-tribe-based club or would it grow into the fulfillment of God's promise to Abraham that *all* nations would be blessed?

   • Why do you think this decision was the most important issue facing the early Jesus-followers?
   • What did the early Christians decide would be the only step (acted out by baptism) that made one part of God's new family?
   • Why was it so important that the Christian community be open to all?

4. Discuss the following statement:

   In the chapter on God's Old Testament family Israel, we made the case that Yahweh handed down some religious laws for a rather subversive reason. He gave them in order to preserve his people *culturally* even as they refused to stand out *morally*. It was by this creative tactic that God would sustain his family until Someone came along to live out the heart of the commandments. Quite simply, Jesus filled that role.

- Why do some Old Testament commands no longer apply to us?
- Describe these older laws with regard to the analogy of sailing ships used to help travelers across the ocean?
- What are some legalistic requirements that Christians today attempt to make central, even when they have little or nothing to do with Scripture?

5. Recall the analogy of the unfinished (Shakespearian) play and discuss the following questions:

- How does the analogy highlight the mission of the church as we tell God's ongoing Story through our lives and actions?
- An actor uses his or her body (Latin: *corpus*) to draw others into a story. How does this relate to the church's mission to be a body (*corpus*) that draws the world into God's Story?
- In the next weeks and months, what can you and your friends begin to do that will reveal God's good news of grace to those who need to hear it most? How can you be the church? Be specific.

NEW CREATION

Why Movies Make Us Cry

For in that sleep of death what dreams may come.

—WILLIAM SHAKESPEARE
HAMLET, ACT III, SCENE 1

My wife's favorite movie is a largely forgotten flick from the late '90s. It's called *What Dreams May Come*. The title comes from Shakespeare. But the film has nothing to do with anyone named Hamlet. The main character is played by a young (and now lamented) Robin Williams. Yet if you've seen the movie, you know it's miles from the comedic shenanigans of *Mrs. Doubtfire*. It's a drama, a sad one, and I don't like those.

The story begins when a family man named Chris Nielson (played by Williams) is killed, along with his children, in a violent auto accident. It's a terrible tragedy, and it leaves only Chris's wife to cope with the anguish of losing her entire family in an instant. It's heart-wrenching. And it becomes more so because, in the film, Chris's ghost is allowed to observe as his wife spirals through a cycle of pain, depression, and ultimately, suicide.

Did I mention that I hate this kind of movie?

Only later does the plot begin to bend in less catastrophic directions. The film is *not* a tragedy. It is a kind of fantasy. Or perhaps, a romance. And it becomes so in a dramatic scene in which the mild-mannered Chris Nielson reaches a decision. He loves his wife. He cannot accept that she is gone forever. He *won't* accept it. And in the movie, he doesn't have to. Despite warnings that rescue is impossible, and despite a verdict that his bride must languish forever in the darkness (supposedly) designed for suicides, Nielson resolves to get her back. He will charge the gates of hell itself if that is what it takes.

And so he does.

The Devil's in the Downy!

If I were *another* kind of Christian writer, I might spend the next pages chumming Bible verses and ranting about how this kind of movie is decidedly unbiblical. The departed can't mount rescue operations to remove the damned from Hades! I could pound my pulpit and go on about how the story presents a picture of heaven and hell that is altogether contrary to Scripture. And

I'd probably be right. "It shows where Hollywood is taking us," I might say. Then I'd follow this rant with a string of e-mail forwards and a proposed boycott of Robin Williams's favorite laundry detergent. We could even coin a slogan. Something catchy like "The devil's in the Downy!"

I could do that, but I'm not going to. Instead, I'm forced to say what happened the last time I watched the move, beside Brianna, all curled up on our fake leather loveseat. What happened was, I cried like a school girl. And not just because I love my wife, or because the film was well done, or because the usually-manic Robin Williams somehow shone brightest in dramatic roles. That's all true. But there is another reason also. I cried, in part, because for whatever reason I found this version of the afterlife compelling. While it may not be the Christian one,[1] still it struck a chord within me. It was gripping and I wondered why.

Perhaps part of the reason stems from the fact that many of our pop notions of the afterlife have left us with some pictures, and frankly some sermons, that just aren't very interesting.

Don't get me wrong, phrases like "heaven" and "eternal life" sound great. But in most cases, they do not sound like an edge-of-your-seat *adventure*. In some cases, they sound comforting, but rather boring. In fact, if you were to ask the average Joe or Jane on the street to describe the hereafter, there is a good chance they would mention a few key elements. They might speak of a place called "heaven" as a location in the sky. A place where people walk on clouds like floors, listen to harp music, and wear halos.

And in fairness, that all sounds nice. After all, relaxation in the sky seems preferable to pounding widgets at a dead-end job. Total peace with harps and halos sounds better than the endless headlines of war and famine. And even the cloud-floor thing sounds better than Grandma's green shag carpeting. It all sounds nice. But it doesn't sound that interesting. And therein lies the problem.

The pop version of the afterlife is just not a movie that I'd want to watch. It actually sounds a little boring. Don't believe me? Try and name something more monotonous than sitting cross-legged on a cloud while Yanni's harpist plays a never-ending PBS special. That's not interesting. And it raises what is, for me, the central question of this final chapter: Why did the (unbiblical) movie make me cry?

After all, I don't cry much. I'm what you'd call *emotionally challenged*. So why did I find this fictional afterlife more compelling than most sermons I have heard on the subject? Here's one possibility.

How to Ruin a Story

I heard recently that the single surefire way to ruin any story is to leave out the one feature that is absolutely essential. No, it's not sex. The crucial feature is *conflict*.[2] According to some literary experts, the indispensable element of any good story is the undeniable sense that there is something at stake, imperiled, or contested.

Something must hang in the balance, and dealing with the conflict determines how things end.

The conflict is what keeps us interested. Without it, we are destined to put down the book, change the channel, or simply walk out of the theater.

Exactly what's at stake is less important. It could be Romeo's love life; it could be the racing rivalry between a certain tortoise against an odds-on favorite hare; or it could be a husband's last-ditch chance to be with his wife. Any of these storylines may work, but the fact remains that something *must* hang in the balance. And if it doesn't, your story will stink.

I heard this conflict theory a while back and it left me wondering if this might be part of the reason why some pop versions of the afterlife leave me yawning. Perhaps they seem less inspired because while the absence of things like death and tears and torture seem wonderful, the apparent absence of adventure, suspense, and yes, even *conflict,* leaves us wondering what there will be to keep us interested.

Admittedly, that seems like an irreverent question. It seems like the kind of question that could get you corrected by the Sunday school teacher. Yet it's with this rather irreverent question in mind that I'd like to revisit what the Scriptures say about the final chapter in God's long and beautiful Story. I'd like to revisit what the Bible actually says about the way our drama culminates. But before we explore what the Bible says, perhaps we should examine what the Bible does not say, and that involves a reference to a certain '80s rock band.

The Apocalypse and Michael Stipe

It was R.E.M. that first sang me a memorable sermon about the end of the world. You may remember it. (If you are a youngster with no memory of that decade, just YouTube it—you'll see what I mean.) It's one of those classic '80s–'90s anthems, and I can still hear it pumping through the tiny factory speakers in my first car, an excrement-brown-colored Toyota Corolla.

The melody (not unlike my car's overworked engine) had a cadence like a machine gun. And the rapid-fire lyrics had a way of worming into your brain. It could get annoying over time, but as far as I know, the song still holds the distinction of being the only rock number to scream the name of "Leonard Bernstein!"

Behind the wordy verses, the theme was *apocalyptic*. It was about the end of the world, and it even came complete with end-times imagery (earthquakes, hurricanes, you get the drift). You might even confuse it for the stuff of cheap Christian fiction. But then there was that little wink at the end of each chorus. It was about the end of the world "as we know it." And as Reverend Stipe was proud to tell us: he felt *fine*.

That last line always stuck out to me. It seemed like an odd way to end. And it made me want to ask the author a question: Excuse me, Mr. Stipe. I'm sorry to interrupt your vocal performance and all, but how is it that you can be so calm? After all, you are singing about the end of the world. How can you feel fine?

I was asking this question one day on the highway, when I came to what I think is a pretty obvious conclusion.

Perhaps when R.E.M. told everyone that the world was coming to a fiery end (spoiler alert), they didn't mean it literally. The song was apocalyptic, yes, but like all good apocalyptic literature (Scripture included), the writer knew his way around a metaphor.

Back to the Bible

This may seem like a silly point to make, but it leads to an important truth. The biblical writers also use imagery that seems, at first glance, to describe the literal end of the space-time world. They speak of the sun turning dark and the moon to blood (see Mark 13:24; Joel 2:31; Acts 2:20). They speak of beasts with horns and epic battles with fire and brimstone. It's intense. And perhaps because of this intensity, we sometimes fail to consider what ought to be obvious. Perhaps the inspired writers of God's Story were at least as skilled in their lyricism as a washed-up '80s rock band.[3]

Scholars tell us it was common practice for biblical prophets and poets to describe earth-shattering events with earth-shattering imagery. In the Bible, everything from the fall of empires, to the destruction of Jerusalem, to the birth and death of kings is portrayed in ways that sound like Armageddon. Startling images are used, *not* necessarily because the writers were foretelling the fiery end of the space-time continuum, but because radical imagery was the only language robust enough to sufficiently convey the magnitude of the spiritual, emotional, and historical situation.

Unfortunately, these passages are easily taken out of context. And this can cause some problems. It causes problems because when it comes time to talk about the return of Jesus and the consummation of God's renewed creation, we are suddenly forced to separate the vivid metaphors from more literal predictions of future events. And that's not easy. Tough questions arise. When is a prophet using apocalyptic imagery to describe, say, the fall of Babylon or Rome, and when is he describing something yet to happen in the distant future? Might he be doing both? It seems so.

There is ambiguity, and much ink has been spilled in the attempt to definitively iron out the mystery of God's future. Every year dozens of (ridiculous) books are sold to people who want the inside scoop on how the world will end.

I was reminded of this a few years back when I walked past a Christian bookstore-souvenir shop in my old hometown. Apparently, the store was making at least some money selling books that claimed to show how Sadaam Hussein (deceased Iraqi dictator and first runner-up for world's greatest mustache) was, in fact, the long-awaited Antichrist. Who knew? The books occupied a huge shelf and sat prominently at the front of the store. They were the first things you saw as you entered and the last thing you saw as you left. On each one was a big sticker telling how the book was fast approaching best-seller status.

So a few months later, when the mustachioed "Antichrist" was caught and executed for crimes against humanity, I decided to return to said bookstore. Not surprisingly, the books had been moved from their coveted shelf space. But I was still able to find one or two copies hastily shoved to the back of the bargain book rack. They were marked down. A lot. For somewhere in the neighborhood of $2.99 you could take home a one-time best seller, or two hundred pages of substandard toilet paper.

Since I was a young theology student at the time, the trip to the bookstore was a lesson learned. It's easy to take creative liberties with apocalyptic imagery. It's a relatively easy way to write books like this, and it's a relatively easy way for publishers to make money. Unfortunately, it's also an easy way to do violence to God's plotline. So before diving into the fictional end-times hoopla, we might do well to remember something from the R.E.M. song.

The biblical writers were lyricists too. They knew a metaphor when they saw one. And even conservative Bible scholars are increasingly ready to admit that some passages once thought to refer to the literal end of the world are, in fact, using vivid metaphors to describe historical events that have already happened (e.g., the fall of Babylon, the fall of Jerusalem, or the persecution of the early church by Rome). At least sometimes.

The warning, then, is simple. While God does have something to say about the consummation of his drama, there's a lot the Bible *doesn't say*. And we would do well to remember that. Speculation may sell books, but it doesn't do justice to God's Story. Now back to the question at hand!

Already

What will new creation be like when it finally comes?

One thing is clear. When the Scriptures speak of this event, they *rarely* speak of an exclusively future occurrence. When the Bible speaks of new creation, it usually speaks of something that has *already* been inaugurated. The startling message of the New Testament is that new creation broke into this old world on the day when Jesus sat up inside a borrowed tomb, wiped the sleep of death from his eyes, and walked confidently into the morning sun.

God's new creation started with the incarnation and, especially, the resurrection. And since Scripture starts there, perhaps we should follow suit.

The new creation message of the Bible is this: what God did for Jesus physically (raising him to eternal life on the third day) God has begun, and will complete, for us as well. Paul says it this way: while we were dead in our sins, God made us alive in Christ (see Colossians 2:13). In other words, while we were spiritually deceased, God raised us to new life in Jesus (see Colossians 3:1). We were walking corpses and God made us alive in the Messiah. And the good news is that our *spiritual renewal* has implications for the physical world as well. Salvation isn't just about beaming our immortal souls to heaven.

To be sure, "heaven" is a real way of speaking about those who have gone to be with Christ upon their death. As Paul puts it, to be absent from our earthly body is to be present with the Lord (see 2 Corinthians 5:8). And as Jesus tells the repentant thief on the cross, "today you will be with me in paradise" (Luke 23:43). So this spiritual existence in heaven is a promise for Christians after death. It's real. As Christ's followers, we go to heaven when we die.

Even so, God's final chapter is even better than this. That's because God's ultimate plan is not about getting your ghost to the Great Beyond so you can sit on a cloud and drink (non-alcoholic?) mojitos. God's final salvation is about renewing the entire physical cosmos as we know it. It involves a bodily resurrection (just like that of Jesus), and as the New Testament hints, aspects of that final resurrection have *already* begun. In a letter to the church in Corinth Paul says it this way: "If anyone is in Christ, the new creation has come" (2 Cor. 5:17).[4]

Take a moment to reread that. Chances are, it may not be quite the translation you are used to. If you're like me, you grew up hearing it like this: "if anyone is in Christ, *he is* a new creation." And while that's certainly true, it is also zooming in the interpretive lens so much as to miss the wider implications of Christ's victory. In the original language, the passage reads more like this: "If anyone is in Messiah: new creation!"

The point is simple. The Scriptures tell us that salvation is not just about what God wants to do for you as an individual (though that's part of it). Salvation is also about what God wants to do *for* the entire created order! That's the hope of the gospel. It's not all about you! It's about an entirely rejuvenated cosmos rising from the ashes of a fallen world.

This is what is so unbiblical about the consumer mentality that sometimes pervades the American church.

Even in our theology it is possible to think of ourselves primarily as customers consuming religious goods and services to meet our personal needs, while all the while missing the entire point of the gospel. I was reminded of this increasingly when I became a pastor and began to strike up conversations with newcomers to our church. When I asked many of these folks what brought them to our gatherings, I was often met with a very interesting response: "We're just *church shopping*."

Church shopping?! Where did we get this phrase? Who taught us to talk about the bride of Jesus like a used Buick?! "Sure she rides nice, but does she come with heated seats?"

Perhaps the saddest thing is that those who use this lingo are not seekers or agnostics. The people who use this phrase are church folks who have been taught that religion is a product to be shopped for like a new pair of jeans. Many of them are nice people, but they have managed to exist for years in a church without ever grasping even the most basic message of the Bible. We exist as Jesus' body, not to be served, but to serve. We have been graciously forgiven by God, so that in gratitude we can spread this grace to others.[5] We enter the Jesus-community to aid the coming of God's renewed creation. That's the point! But somewhere amid our wealth and privilege, many of us (myself included) have missed it.

New creation began when the lungs of Jesus took their first breath inside a damp and darkened tomb. And new creation continues with us. It continues when we take our first breath of God's transforming Spirit.[6] But there is one more step to come. New creation also awaits a future fulfillment. It has begun *already*, but it is *not yet* finished. And it's toward the *not yet* that we now turn.

Not Yet

The flipside of new creation is this: the world is still fallen. It still groans out as in the pains of childbirth. We still smell the stench of sin and death around us and within us. It's present everywhere and it often seems to rule the day. Pain is everywhere and it leads us to ask an honest question: If God's new creation really has begun, then why doesn't it seem like it?

It's a question that God's people have asked in different ways for centuries. It's difficult, but the best answer we possess is this: at the moment God's kingdom exists largely undercover. We see it breaking in from time to time: in a church family that chooses to swim against the stream of consumerism and racial division, in a married couple that chooses the path of forgiveness when they want to just give up, or in a businessperson who chooses to use his or her wealth on something more redemptive than just a bigger house and nicer clothes. We see new creation breaking in through things like this, yet we still await a final decisive act to bring it into its fullness.

We still need rescue, and the hope of God's last chapter is that rescue *is* coming. Jesus *will* return. The Scriptures promise it (see, for instance, Acts 1:11). But when he does, it won't be just to extract cowering saints from the rubble of a forsaken planet. It won't be to evacuate a bunch of me-focused consumers so we can live on a cloud. This is the story of religious dualism. It's *not* the story of the Bible. The story of the Bible is that Jesus will come *down*—down into the heart of this beautiful disaster—and make known his indisputable victory over evil. New creation will come in full. And when it does, the created world—the world of California Redwoods, Michigan microbrews, and Miles Davis music—will be transformed.[7] This world will not be flicked away like a smoked-down cigarette. It will be renewed. Now a word on that.

Booing the President

Several years ago, I had a run-in with a certain U.S. president. Exactly *which* president is not important, but it happened when the chief executive decided to pay a visit to the town where Brianna and I were living. The visit was supposed to be somewhat of a surprise, but just a few days before, the local media broke the news that the leader of the free world was dropping by to speak at a local middle school.

Unfortunately, the leader of the free world neglected to invite me to his speech. I'm over it, but the snub meant that for me "the big day" was just *Friday*. And Friday was my day off. As such, it usually began with a trip to my favorite coffeehouse and a morning filled with two of my favorite things—chemically induced euphoria (i.e., dark coffee) and one-sided conversations with dead people (old books).

That's what I was up to when the president came. I spent the morning at my favorite coffee bar, before leaving for home and lunch.

Except this day I couldn't get home. I couldn't make it because as I pulled our teal Chevy Cavalier out of the parking lot (yes, I graduated from brown excrement to teal), I quickly realized that virtually every street had been cordoned off for you-know-who. He's such an attention hog. My quiet drive looked a bit like a parade route. Police were everywhere. And it was then that I saw them.

They had signs and they were yelling angry things that I couldn't hear at first. Apparently, they hadn't been invited to the speech either. Some of them had even composed special artwork for the occasion, mostly stick figures and exclamation points. Upon listening closer, I could hear them chanting about a war, some lies, and about some other things I couldn't quite make out. They wanted the president to see them, and they wanted him to know that they weren't happy. They wanted him to know that while he may have expected a warm reception, he wasn't going to get one. Things weren't being run the way they wanted, and the presidential visit was a chance to let people know.

Greeting the King

When I finally made it home that day, I thought about the way the Bible describes the so-called second coming of Jesus. Specifically, I thought of a passage written by Paul. It goes like this:

> For the Lord himself will come down from heaven, with a loud command, with the voice of the archangel and with the trumpet call of God,

and the dead in Christ will rise first. After that,
we who are still alive and are left will be caught
up together with them in the clouds to meet the
Lord in the air. And so we will be with the Lord
forever. (1 Thess. 4:16–17)

It's an important passage. And a few things are clear:
Jesus *will* return; the dead in Christ will rise to new life;
and we will be with the Lord, forever.

Unfortunately, what is perhaps easiest to miss
in Paul's metaphorical language is the very analogy
that he wants to bring to mind. Despite appearances,
I don't think that he is speaking about a kind of *Star
Trek*-inspired rapture in which Christians are beamed
up to heaven while non-Christians are left behind on
earth. Despite what many (mostly American) Christians
believe on this, there is little basis for the view in either
Christian history or the Bible itself. It is virtually nonex-
istent in the first nineteen centuries of the church, and it
is never taught explicitly within the Scriptures. In short,
Paul isn't talking about an evacuation. Paul is talking
about a royal return that will bring about the renewal of
our fallen world.[8]

In the passage, he is comparing the return of Jesus
to the return of an emperor (or king) to a city that is
suffering. And, interestingly enough, it is just this kind
of visit with which the letter's original recipients (Jesus-
followers in a town called Thessalonica) would have been
familiar.

Here's how it worked. In such times, a once-proud
city would be ravaged by famine or fire or earthquake.

Scores would be killed, buildings would be decimated, and the social fabric of the community would be torn apart. Yet despite the best efforts of the citizens to rebuild and restore things on their own, the obstacles were sometimes too great. Not all problems can be solved by pulling ourselves up by the bootstraps and just trying harder. What such ancient people needed in this scenario was the renewal and rebuilding that only their lord (a common title for the Roman Caesar) could provide.

And occasionally, if the lord was feeling generous, he would come.

As the lord and king approached, the tired citizens would be so ecstatic that they would not wait inside the shattered city. They could not wait. So they would go to greet their ruler *outside the gates*. They would leave their homes and neighborhoods and they would meet their sovereign beyond the city limits. Here, they would welcome him, not with picket signs and accusations, but with thanksgiving. The lord had finally come to Thessalonica, and the people would rush out to meet him.

But then the ruler would do something important. Rather than order the citizens to relocate elsewhere. And rather than simply pitching a tent beyond the city's broken gates, the Roman lord would make a unilateral decision. He would march back into the ravaged city with its citizens, and *together* they would start anew. The lord and his subjects would return together to the place where death and destruction had reigned and the ruler would make things right.

Many scholars agree that *this* is the imagery Paul draws upon when describing the return of King Jesus. It will be like a presidential visit, he says, like a *royal visit* to a disaster zone—but with a crucial difference! Rather than greeting our King with picket signs and angry rhetoric, God's people will join their Lord (whether figuratively or not) "in the air"—beyond the earthen boundaries of our ravaged creation. And together we will return *with Jesus* to rebuild the ruins of God's good creation.[9]

This is the point proclaimed by the entire storyline of Scripture: Jesus is not leading an evacuation movement! He is not leading a retreat! And he is *not* coming back to take us away! The return of the Messiah is not a relocation to an immaterial heaven where we live as ghosts. It is not a last-minute extraction from a napalm-smelling war zone. No! Jesus is coming to renew the broken world that he loves—and we are called to join the effort. This is the promise of a renewed creation. *Everything* will be made new, and we will be with our Lord, forever.

What about Hell?

In all of this, the careful reader will note that I have not yet made even a single mention of a place called "hell." There is a reason for this omission. We stated at the outset that our goal was to tell the story of God's people, and for God's people, hell has no place.

In several places, the Bible does indicate that there will be some who willingly reject King Jesus.[10] There will be some—including some religious types—who spend their lives undermining God's actual purposes, subverting God's agenda, and standing like angry protestors before the King of kings. If we are honest with the Scriptures, we cannot deny this—no amount of fancy Greek word studies can get you out of it.[11] Our King does not force anyone to enjoy his presence. And if there are those who have hated the way of Jesus in this life, we have no reason to expect that they will suddenly enjoy it in the age to come.

But with this conclusion, comes also a caution. As Christ-followers, we must reject the temptation to pronounce judgment on who is definitively "in" and who is "out." That's not our job! The text makes that much clear.[12] And if God's surprising storyline has taught us anything, it is that grace has a way of exceeding our narrow religious expectations.[13] It is not our duty is to track attendance in God's final kingdom. Our duty is to live in such a way as to make way for the King. Because he's coming back.

This is the same message found in the often-confusing book of Revelation. Here we are bowled over by the imagery of a beautiful city (the renewed Jerusalem), coming *down* out of heaven. (Note: it's coming down!) And it's at the sight of this symbolic city that the writer hears words that fall like rain on parched soil:

> And I heard a loud voice from the throne saying, "Look! God's dwelling place is now among the people, and he will dwell with them. They will be his people, and God himself will be with them and be their God. 'He will wipe every tear from their eyes. There will be no more death' or mourning or crying or pain, for the old order of things has passed away." He who was seated on

the throne said, "I am making everything new!"
(Rev. 21:3–5)

This is the good news of God's final chapter. After many twists of plot along the way, after many failures and false steps, the great drama turns out well! And on the edge of new creation, we will look backward and appreciate the artistry.

The story starts in a garden. In the beginning, a pair of happy honeymooners are asked to care for God's good world. They are asked to do something with it—something constructive. But they fail. The Story starts with a garden. But the Story *ends* in a city. Even so, it is not the kind of city in which smog and concrete cover green and growing things. It's a garden city, with rivers and minerals, light and leaves—and the tree of life (see Revelation 22). The story ends with God bringing order to chaos and building with his hands what we could not build alone. The story ends with a glimmering city coming down to rest on the earthen soil of a once-broken world.

The plotline ends with a promise that in spite of all our faults and failures—our youthful indiscretions and our aged priggishness—the Creator God is making *everything* new. Revelation tells us this, and it ends with an announcement: "Behold, our Lord is coming soon!" (Rev. 22:12). He is coming, and new creation is coming with him.

A Ridiculous Question

In retrospect, perhaps this is a smart place to conclude. After all, it's where the Bible ends things. Revelation stops with the picture of a renewed cosmos coming fully to a fallen world. It sounds wonderful, and—again—it is probably a smart place to conclude. Yet we started this chapter with a more peculiar question.

The question had to do with *life* in God's new creation. What will it be like? What makes heaven, *heaven*? And more provocatively: If conflict really is the spice of every earthly story—the necessary ingredient of all narratives—what will hold our attention in a conflict-free world?

The temptation, of course, is to avoid this final question by calling it absurd. Perhaps it is. It certainly invites your criticism. "Who cares if there is no conflict?! Is that such a big deal? Is it really such a tragedy to picture heaven as little more than an endless church service, an eternal reunion, or a never-ending vacation? Is that so terrible?!"

Perhaps not. In truth, the generic pop notion of heaven isn't terrible, but it is incomplete. In fact, some pseudo-Christian notions of the afterlife seem lacking for a simple reason. They are lacking because in some cases they cease to view God as he is *in the beginning*. And in so doing, they change his nature.

Further Up, Further In

Think back. When we first meet the God of the Bible, what exactly is he up to? The writer of Genesis says that in the beginning God is *creating*. In other words, the Creator isn't sitting idly by and enjoying a celestial nap. He isn't basking in the amenities of a heavenly Club Med. When we first meet God, he is creating.

When we first meet God, he is painting new worlds on the canvas of a cosmos he created. He is dipping Word and Spirit into the colors of creation. Like a Playwright, he is shaping a drama from the overflow of his imagination. He is endlessly generative. His love and glory flame forth inherently. How could they not? In the beginning, God is creating.

Yet when many of us picture life with this same God at the end of the drama, the primary images that we conjure up are not particularly creative: people sitting by on clouds; a kind of heavenly all-inclusive resort; easy-listening praise and worship; three chords and redundancy. It isn't terrible. But it isn't that *creative*.

C. S. Lewis seemed to have a problem with this notion of eternity as well. As a storyteller himself, perhaps Lewis had a hard time picturing life in God's new creation in ways that were the least bit boring. (Perhaps writers are more attuned to such matters. We know almost instinctively that God's plotline—however it goes—must be *more interesting* than our own.) For Lewis, life in God's renewed world was never about sitting around on cloud floors with harps and halos. In his mind, life with God was about movement, exploration, and adventure. It was about God's creatures worshipping him and enjoying his new world by moving "further up and further in!"

This was the phrase Lewis used. "Further up and further in!" At its core, it was a call for humans to set out on a new adventure into God's new world. It was a call to bid farewell to the *shadowlands* and to dive into a deeper country in which we will worship the creative Creator by exploring, enjoying, and at all times glorifying the One who made us for himself. For Lewis, this was life in God's new creation. It was a sacred adventure in which humans were allowed to experience the universe as it was always meant to be.

For Lewis, heaven was not the end of the drama. Heaven was the beginning. It was: "Chapter One of the Great Story which no one on earth has read: which goes on forever: in which every chapter is better than the one before."[14]

Why Movies Make Us Cry

Perhaps this sheds some light on our original inquiry about what makes stories work. We started this chapter with a single loaded question: If conflict is the spice of every good story *now*, what of life in God's new creation? If there is no conflict, can there still be joy?

I think there can.

The reason goes back, if you can believe it, to the strange movie that we spoke of at the beginning of this chapter. The one that was so decidedly unbiblical. Or, if you prefer, the one that made me cry.

Movies do that sometimes. They do it to my wife a lot. We'll be sitting in the soft seats at the theater and I'll hear her start to sniffle. (Then the preview will end and she'll cheer up when the talking soda cup comes dancing out to tell everyone to silence their cell phones.) It's cute.

But movies are not the only things that make us cry. There are other things: the birth of a child, the images of soldiers coming home from war, even the way a singer wraps her voice around a melody. Such things can make us emotional, *not* because they are sad, but because they awaken a certain universal ache inside of us.

I was thinking about that ache awhile back. Specifically, it was during an episode of that old TV show where people would makeover houses and then give them away like giant fruit baskets. And I've developed a theory about what's going on there.

Suppose for a second that it isn't conflict specifically that makes us care about a story. Oh, conflict is involved of course. But suppose the real reason we are drawn to this spice is that we possess a universal sense that somehow, someday, every conflict must be swallowed up in joy. Perhaps that's why we're drawn to art that bleeds with dissonance. Perhaps that's why even I cry sometimes. And not always in sadness. It isn't the conflict itself that draws us. Rather, it's the primal notion that one day every tear will be wiped away.

When that happens, a door will open on a greater story. And in this story, something greater than conflict will hold our attention. Far from being bored, we will spend our days striving to get closer to the Someone who took the ache away. We will want to thank this Someone, fall at his feet, and spend eons wrapped in the mystery of redemption.

No, it isn't conflict that keeps us interested. It isn't conflict at all. It is the aching sense that one day every conflict will be swallowed up in love. Perhaps this is the root of every earthly joy. Maybe the reason we love anything in this world is that it carries but an echo of the world to come. Morning is coming and we ache to see the light. That's why movies make us cry. We see the glimmer of eternity in the face of a child, in the bend of a melody, or in the arc of a film—and we know it's coming. There's another chapter breaking in. And in that everlasting light of life, what dreams may come?

Engage the Story

Having read about the new creation chapter in God's Story, it's time now to engage with it yourself. Read the following passages this week, reflect upon their meaning, and be prepared to discuss them with others:

- 1 Thessalonians 4:13–5:11
- Revelation 4
- Revelation 21–22

Discuss the Story

1. The final chapter in God's Story has to do with an entirely renewed creation. It could be argued that this is the hardest chapter to talk about because, for now, we live in a world that is still broken and longing for renewal. For evidence of this, read Romans 8:18–22 together and discuss the following questions:

   - As you look around, how do you see the "groaning" of creation?
   - Despite this groaning, how do you see new creation breaking in through the work of God's Spirit and God's people?
   - A more literal translation of 2 Corinthians 5:17 states that "if anyone is in the Messiah—new creation!" What does the verse seem to imply

about the results of God's grace in the lives of his people? Have you ever thought of yourself as an agent of God's new creation?

2. The Bible arguably compares the return of Jesus to the return of a king to his suffering city. To see this imagery, read 1 Thessalonians 4:16–17 together and then discuss the following questions:

- Why do you think this passage is sometimes used to make the argument that Jesus is coming back only to whisk us all away from this dirty and evil world?
- How does the author confront this perspective with a different possibility?

3. Some Christians make it sound as if our ultimate hope in life is that our immaterial soul would float up to heaven when we die. Without denying the reality of heaven after we die, this chapter politely challenges the notion that an immaterial evacuation is our ultimate hope. Here is the two-fold progression:

A. After death, we can trust that we will indeed be "with the Lord" where he is—hence, we "go to heaven" (see 2 Corinthians 5:8; John 14:2; Luke 23:43; Philippians 1:23; Revelation 6:9–11).

B. Even so, the ultimate end to God's Story includes the resurrection of our physical bodies, and the renewal of God's good creation (see 1 Thessalonians 4:16–17; John 5:25–29; Daniel 12:13).

- Does this two-stage view of the afterlife differ from the one you may have been taught previously?

- What is wrong with the idea that God's creative project will ultimately be burned up and disregarded?

4. The Bible ends with the imagery of a beautiful new civilization (the "New Jerusalem") coming down out of heaven, so that all things are made new. Read Revelation 21:2–5 and discuss the following questions:

   - Why does the chapter stress the fact that the city in the image is coming down?
   - Many biblical writers longed for the day when God would bring his justice to a fallen world. Do you often find yourself longing for God to come and set this world right? How so?
   - For those undergoing persecution, injustice, or illness, the hope of God's new creation is often what gives courage to continue living, working, and loving in the midst of difficult times. Have you ever experienced this in your own life? Why do you think it is that some affluent and healthy Westerners may long for God's new creation in less obvious ways than, say, Christians in other parts of the world?

5. This chapter makes the case that it is our hope in the resurrection that ought to provide us with the motivation to get off our butts and go to work for God as he begins to renew this world. Some individuals might hold the opposite view (that is, because God is going to destroy this world soon, we shouldn't worry too much about *earthly* matters such as economic justice or environmental stewardship.)

- Have you ever encountered something like this perspective?
- How would you answer a religious person who articulated a viewpoint not unlike the negative one above?
- Why is it important that God called his creation "good" to begin with, especially when we consider the ultimate fate of the physical world?

6. Recall C. S. Lewis's idea that the reason we love anything in this life is because it carries a glimmer of the life to come.

   That's why movies make us cry. We see the glimmer of eternity from time to time, in the face of a child, in the bend of a melody, or in the arc of a film, and we know it is coming. There is another chapter breaking in, and we know it. The Story ends well for God's people, and this is just the beginning.

   - Spend some time prayerfully reflecting on this thought.
   - In closing, you may want to pray together one of the final phrases in God's Story. For instance: "Come, Lord Jesus" (Rev. 22:20). Bring about the beautiful conclusion to your Story that we have all been waiting for. Rescue this world from sin and death and use us to be a part of that rescue! Amen.

CONCLUSION

Why the Beatles Want to Fish

Not long ago, I read a *Rolling Stone* interview with John Lennon. While I don't subscribe to the magazine, the conversation was published in a book containing dozens of interviews done by the publication over the years. All the great ones were there: Cash, Dylan, Springsteen. But I remember Lennon best. It was the first interview that the former Beatle allowed after deciding to leave the biggest rock band in the world. "Why'd you do it?" was the question everyone was asking. "How in God's name could you say good-bye to the kind of universal fame that every garage-band dreams about? How could you just up and walk away? How could you do this to us?!"

I'm not a Beatles' junkie. But as I read through the dialogue between the artist and the interviewer, I couldn't help but see Lennon's commentary as a rather honest reflection on the perils of life in the limelight. Fame can be a cancer. And at one point, the reporter asked the rock star a fascinating question:

"Would you take it all back?"

"What?" asked Lennon.

"Being a Beatle?"

The musician paused for a long moment. Then he answered: "If I could be a [bleepin'] fisherman, I would."[1]

At first glance, it seems like a strange admission. "You know, I think I'd like to go catch tuna for a living." Maybe shrimp. After all, that Lieutenant Dan from *Forest Gump* seemed pretty happy at the Bubba Gump Shrimp Company—and he had no legs! But that wasn't quite what Lennon meant.

What he meant was, if I could go back and rewrite my story, I'd do it differently. In fact, if I could delete the chapters that made me an icon, a celebrity, a god—I would. I'd go back and replace all that stuff with chapters from another story—maybe even one in which I spent my days trawling salmon off the coast of Alaska. That can't be bad, right? No cameras following you into the bathroom, no managers telling you to sell your soul to fit a niche. No hype.

That's what Lennon was thinking. "If I could insert myself into a different story, I'd do it. I'd be a [bleepin'] fisherman, not a Beatle."

Your Place in the Story

His answer strikes at the only reason why my book should matter to you. It should matter for the simple reason that far too many people—plumbers, mothers, teachers, salesmen—feel a bit like Lennon. We're not as rich or as famous. But that doesn't change the problem.

All of us have wished at one point or another that we could be part of a more fulfilling story. We've wished, at least once, that we would have taken a different path in life, chosen a different major in college, a different spouse, or a different set of friends. We've wished that we hadn't wasted so much time trying to fit in, trying to be popular, or climbing the corporate ladder.

We all want to be a part of a story that grants real significance. We want to die knowing that our life had meaning beyond a paycheck and a Facebook profile. We want to sense that we were a part of something larger than ourselves, and that it wasn't just a waste of time.

And from time to time, when life slows down, we realize that this fulfillment doesn't come by making money, selling records, or even seeing a lot of beautiful people naked. It just doesn't. Ask Lennon. Ask anyone who's ever made it. The truth is: fame is shallow, beauty fades, and dollars die with you. It's not melodramatic. It's just the truth. And from time to time we sense this reality, whether we are rock stars or housewives. And when it hits us, another realization comes close behind. You don't just need a better job, a thinner spouse, or stronger meds—you need a better story. You need to be a part of a story that actually matters.

The Scriptures give us a glimpse of that plotline. And it's the only reason that my book matters. It matters only if it points you toward a Story that is big and true and beautiful enough to give you meaning. It matters only if it reveals for you God's Story: revealed in creation, the fall, Israel, Jesus, church, and new creation.

1. Creation

In the beginning of this drama, we meet an Artist-God creating *from* and *for* community. He creates from and for loving, personal relationships. In a world charged with conflict, the Scriptures paint a portrait of a universe born out of an embrace:

Father, Son, and Spirit;
Adam, Eve, and earth;
Stars and angels singing;
Creation and Creator.

God's Story begins with the kind of authentic belonging that many of us can only imagine. Rather than giving us a scientific text on exactly how and when the world came to be, the Scriptures offer us a glimpse into the soul of creative community. Father speaking, Spirit brooding, Son begotten like a Word of life. It is a picture of life the way it was meant to be: naked communion.

And because our story starts this way, we are forced to grapple with the fact that God designed us to live deeply together. Rugged individualism may be the foundation of the American ethos, but it is fundamentally contrary to the God who is Trinity. We cannot take the Bible seriously and at the same time talk about a spirituality that revolves around "just me and Jesus." This has nothing to do with the script of Scripture. Our script begins in an embrace. Chapter 1 may teach us many other things, but this one thing is certain: we were made *from* and *for* a kind of holy, loving communion.

2. The Fall

Chapter 2 is about the way communion falls apart. Unfortunately, this part of the story is often told in such a way as to make the Creator look like a legalistic schoolmaster, taunting people with forbidden fruit and then punishing them when the apple goes off like an A-bomb in their faces.

This is one way to view the fall. But there is a better one.

We might see the "apple" as an opportunity.[2] From this perspective, God's command about the tree and the fruit is not a pointless bit of religious legalism but an opportunity for humanity to crush the head of evil before it worms its way into everything. As guardians of God's good garden, Adam and Eve are called to exercise the will of their King—to image him, and to rule as he would. They are given the authority and the occasion to do what the tale's audience would know was to be done to traitors under trees. They are called to judge the evil one.

But as we often do, humans stumble in the story, and an opportunity is squandered. In distrusting God, we find that we can no longer trust each other. Sin enters the equation and community unravels. Genesis 3–11 shows how things fall apart both then and now. And for each of us, the story is familiar. The fall is not just about something that happened; it is also about something that happens now, to us.[3]

The story of the fall reads like a chapter in our own biography. It reminds us of our own sins, missteps, and missed opportunities. As Paul says, "we have all sinned and fallen short" (Rom. 3:23). Because of this, none of us have the right to claim the exclusive moral high ground. We've fallen too. And this knowledge serves to guard against the kind of (Christian) arrogance that comes so easily.

Chapter 2 is a call to humility and repentance. The good news, however, is that the fall is not the final chapter. Because as we said, in the Scriptures, not even talking serpents get the final say.

3. Israel

As the dust settles over Genesis 3–11, a rescue operation is in the works. The third movement in our grand Story begins when God does something unexpected to bring about redemption. What he uses is a (somewhat) dysfunctional family. The Creator calls the children of Abraham to be the bringers of his hope. He marries himself to them through a covenant and calls them Israel. As a people, they must wrestle with the unfathomable reality that they have been blessed to bless the nations. God chooses the one for the sake of the many.

But there is a problem with God's family. They are just like us. They are fickle and selfish and broken. They wander to Egypt but end up enslaved. They are delivered but end up grumbling about the food. They have a covenant but want a king. So like a jilted lover who just won't let go, God gives his beloved people what they want.

Over the centuries, the wrestlers repeat a familiar pattern of exile and return; penalty and repentance. There are bouts of faithfulness and bouts of rejection. Israel is called back to God by prophets and poets. Yet, in time, a sad reality becomes apparent. Despite their best attempts, the wrestlers themselves are still in need of rescuing.

The family called to bring the solution to sin and evil has itself become part of the problem. Israel is unable to keep the heart of God's law and, in so doing, she alternates between fits of idolatry, exploitation, and religious pride. One day she wants to be like the pagan neighbors, the next she wants to see them burn. We are like the Israelites in this, and like them, we need rescuing.

Over time, a painful fear begins to break upon God's people like an ocean wave. Perhaps it was too much to think that rescue could come through Israel. Perhaps old man Abram misheard. Perhaps the whole story was simply a myth. Perhaps. But amid the doubts and questions, something peculiar happens. Under the boot of yet another pagan superpower (Rome), an unmarried Jewish teenager gets pregnant. And the rescue takes an unexpected turn.

4. Jesus

In the birth of Christ, the Creator steps into the storyline. As an Israelite himself, he will fulfill the promise that rescue would come through this unlikely family.

And when we glimpse God in the face of Jesus, all we know of religion must be readjusted. In most cultures, the gods were but monstrous amplifications of human power, violence, and vindictiveness. Yet in a Galilean Jew, divinity becomes small and humble.[4]

God becomes a Jewish peasant, and his lineage proves the purpose of calling forth this family in the first place. Through the Law and Prophets and all who went before, the Creator was cultivating a culture in which the work of his Son might be made intelligible. Jesus comes as an Israelite, but in another sense, he comes as Israel. He is the true Israel, the Suffering Servant, the true representative of all humanity. He is the Second Adam, and he must do what God's people could not do alone. He must face down sin and death, absorb them in his broken body, and reveal what it looks like for God's kingdom to come on earth as it is in heaven.

Through the broken-and-resurrected body of Jesus, God wins the decisive victory over sin, death, and the devil. In his life, death, and resurrection, the entire narrative pivots into a whole new phase. In this phase, evil still lives but as a kind of death-row criminal whose time is short. Its fate is sealed as we glimpse our future in the resurrection of the Messiah.

By living as a peaceful revolutionary, Jesus reveals what our own lives must look like. We must be advocates for justice and compassion. We must confront the three-fold evils of religious pride, pagan self-indulgence, and imperial arrogance. We must spend ourselves on behalf of others and in so doing we must imitate the way of our Savior. We must be his body.

5. Church

There is, however, a problem with being God's body. We are not like God. We are sinful, and we tend to act more like the dysfunctional family of the Old Testament than the carpenter from Nazareth. We may be forgiven, but we are still broken. And most days, the brokenness is readily apparent. In other words, we have a tendency to become a part of the problem too.

For this reason, the fifth movement in God's plotline is about the gift with the power to transform ordinary fishermen, plumbers, and gym teachers into entirely new people. The gift is God's Breath. Or, if you prefer, his Holy Spirit.

Through the coming of the Spirit at Pentecost, the Jesus community is empowered to reach out to a world that does not know the news about King Jesus.[5] We are made new (over time) both internally and externally. As believers, we are blown by this Wind toward a more loving and generous existence. The Bible calls this "holiness." And as it did for the first disciples, God's Breath compels us to set aside our prejudices in favor of a new reality: the ever-expanding family of God. While membership in this family used to involve an ethnic and national identity, now there is but one stipulation: allegiance to King Jesus.

Just as it did for the early Christians, God's Holy Spirit compels us to speak the language of outsiders, to be bold yet humble, and to invite even the most unlikely folks to join the revolution. In this way, the church is not a business, but a body. We are not a corporation, but the *corpus Christi* here on earth. As Christ's body, our mission is not just saving souls for heaven, but joining the Spirit of the Creator-God in renewing the totality of creation here on earth: everything from economics to agriculture, foreign policy to after-school programs. In these and other ways, the Spirit goes about the quiet work of making all things new. And just as it was within the book of Acts, this humble work of restoration often goes unnoticed by the powerful and proud. But it is no less real because of that.

6. New Creation

We are motivated to live this life of reckless love because we believe in the resurrection—not just that of Jesus, but of ourselves and of our world too. While some may be content to hunker down under the protective bubble of the Christian subculture until a time when Jesus beams us up, the Scriptures speak of something quite different with regard to the final chapter in God's Story. In addition to being with Christ (spiritually) upon death, the Scriptures also speak of a day when God's kingdom will come fully on earth as it is in heaven. The earth itself, as Isaiah said, "will be filled with the knowledge of the LORD as the waters cover the sea" (11:9). And on this day, all things will be made new. This is the hope of new creation.

We await the return of Jesus, not because it provides a chance to be whisked away from this evil world, but because it promises the redemption of God's broken creation. Evil will be judged, and truth will be vindicated.

As Paul states: "the dead in Christ will rise" and "we will be with the Lord forever" (1 Thess. 4:16–17).

History will end in the embrace of loving community. There will be a celebration. Wine and worship will flow together at a marriage feast. And we will praise the Creator who brought beauty out of chaos and crafted the greatest drama of them all: the Story of redemption.

We read the Scriptures to find our place within the messy masterpiece. But just knowing the movements isn't enough. The goal is not accumulating answers for Bible trivia. The goal is living in such a way as to join the Hero in seeing things end well. Because whether we know it or not, the Author is moving the composition to its beautiful conclusion.

When that happens, our common hope will be realized. The same ache that once drew us into stories of all kinds will be healed. The deep human fissure will be mended. And on that day a greater story will begin. The page will turn in God's grand novel, and we will spend our days in headlong pursuit of the One who "reconciles the ill-matched threads of our lives and weaves them gratefully into a single cloth."[6]

NOTES

Introduction

1. Our word for "Bible" comes from the Latin: *biblia* (literally: "books").
2. Though we use this analogy quite differently, it was Brian McLaren who first introduced the Bible-as-puzzle metaphor to me in a live talk I attended in 2008.
3. The idea of Scripture as a "script in search of actors" is drawn appreciatively from the many works of N. T. Wright.
4. This six-chapter model is not entirely unique to me, nor is it sacred in and of itself. There are other ways of dividing up the Story that may work just as well. The current model owes much to the more in-depth work of N. T. Wright, as well as the other thinkers and theologians cited as follows. For a slightly more academic rendering of the six-part drama, see Craig G. Bartholomew and Michael Goheen, *The Drama of Scripture: Finding Our Place in the Biblical Story,* 2nd ed. (Grand Rapids, MI: Baker Academic, 2014).

Chapter One

1. The story in question is a Babylonian creation myth entitled *Enuma Elish*. It dates (according to some scholars) to the second millennium BC.
2. To be fair to Job's wife (or at least fairer than most Christian commentators have been), no one would

likely suffer more from Job's death than she. Thus, when she commands Job to "curse God and die," we cannot be sure of her true motives. Did she blame Job for her children's deaths? Did she merely want to end Job's pain? Or was she just playing out the script that so many of us have at one time or another: hurting people hurt people?

3. The Old Testament scholar John Walton argues that the very language that is used of Eden and creation in Genesis is meant to evoke the idea of an ancient temple. Just as the presence of a deity was seen to "rest" (or inhabit) a temple via his "image" (idol), so too God "rests" and inhabits his creation, in part, through his image-bearers (humanity). See especially John H. Walton, *The Lost World of Genesis One: Ancient Cosmology and the Origins Debate* (Downers Grove, IL: IVP, 2009).

4. It is somewhat controversial in theological circles to refer to the Trinity as a "community." The understandable fear in such language is that it tends inherently toward tri-theism (the belief that there are three gods to be worshipped). While this danger must be avoided, there is precedent in the Christian tradition for speaking of the one God as an eternal *koinonia* "communion." This is so especially in the Cappadocian Fathers of the fourth century—who helped the church to articulate the doctrine of the Trinity: One God, existing eternally in three persons: Father, Son, and Holy Spirit.

5. For more witty insights on faith, life, and circus sideshows, see Donald Miller, *Searching for God Knows What* (Nashville, TN: Thomas Nelson, 2004), 61.

6. On the distinction between guilt and shame, see the work of Brené Brown. A helpful introduction to this work can be found in her (viral) TED Talk, "Listening to Shame."

Chapter Two

1. C. S. Lewis, *Mere Christianity* (New York: Macmillan, 1952), 46.
2. John Milton, *Paradise Lost.* Book IV, Line 370.
3. This is close to a famous (and perhaps apocryphal) quote from the theologian Karl Barth. When asked by a woman whether the Genesis-serpent actually spoke, he was reported to have replied: "Madam, it doesn't matter if the serpent spoke. What matters is what the serpent said." As with the parables of Jesus, God-breathed truth does not always have to come by way of rigid literalism. Cited in N. T. Wright, *Simply Christian: Why Christianity Makes Sense* (New York: Harper One, 2006), 183.
4. For whatever it's worth, Genesis never claims that the talking serpent is perched within the branches of the fateful tree. The scene is just easier to paint this way.
5. Deuteronomy 21:22–23 hints at the ancient practice of desecrating the bodies of convicts by hanging them from trees. The fact that the Scriptures take time to discourage this practice only corroborates the historical and anthropological evidence that such things were occurring among neighboring peoples. It also bears noting that some Old Testament judges (namely Deborah in Judges 4) would set up court under a prominent tree. I am indebted to my Torah professor, Dr. Gordon Hugenburger, for pointing out this textual possibility as it pertains to Genesis 3.
6. This is how the prophet Jeremiah describes it: "[God's] people have committed two sins: They have forsaken me, the spring of living water, and have dug their own cisterns, broken cisterns that cannot hold water" (2:13).
7. As we'll see in later chapters, this does not mean that keeping God's commands is what makes us right with

God. Only grace, poured out through Jesus Christ, can do that. Nor does it mean that the Law does not have some shady side effects when it comes into contact with our fallen human nature. Stay tuned.

8. G. K. Chesterton, *As I Was Saying,* ed. Robert Knille (Grand Rapids, MI: Eerdmans, 1985), 160; cited in C. John Collins, "Adam and Eve as Historical People, and Why It Matters," in *Perspectives on Science and Christian Faith,* 62 (Sept. 2010), 158.

9. Exactly how the effects of sin spread to humanity at large is somewhat disputed among theologians. Some think that it was simply passed on genetically, from Adam to his offspring. Another view, however, sees the result of sin as a kind of spiritual radiation that spread outward from the blast, and enveloped the whole cosmos. Either way, the Christian view is that the whole world is now fractured, despite its abiding goodness and beauty.

Chapter Three

1. See Thomas Cahill, *The Gifts of the Jews: How a Tribe of Desert Nomads Changed the Way Everyone Thinks and Feels* (New York: Doubleday, 1998), 60.

2. At the heart of God's promise to Abraham and his family is the ancient Hebrew concept of *covenant*. In this covenant, the Creator enters into a binding relationship with the family of Abram in order to deal with the problem of sin. Things went bad in the garden, and this covenant relationship is God's way of beginning to set the world right. Through Abraham's family, God will ultimately bless the whole world and bring glory to his name.

3. Of course, this way of putting things only shows Jacob's blessing from a human perspective. From the perspective of God's sovereign plan, it was Yahweh who chose

to work through the younger brother rather than the older one.

4. The Hebrew word for "heel" is *aqeb*; hence "Jacob" (*yaqob*) is a play on it. While the name does not literally mean "deceiver," the image of Jacob grasping at that which is not rightfully his (at least by birth) gives rise to his labeled identity as a deceptive grasper.

5. My phrasing of "election" as "one for the sake of the others" is indebted to Colin Gunton, on whose work I did my PhD thesis.

6. The professor's name was James H. Cone. His most famous work is *The Cross and the Lynching Tree* (Maryknoll, NY: Orbis, 2011). While I hardly agree with all of Cone's conclusions, the plea to read the Scriptures from the perspective of the oppressed is crucial. And there are indeed connections between the cross and the "lynching tree."

7. The Hebrew word for "holy" designates something that is *set apart* for God.

8. This does not imply that we may simply ignore any Old Testament commands that our modern preferences find unsavory. We will address this question more fully in chapters 5 and 6. For a more detailed exploration of cultural versus transcultural issues within the Bible, see William J. Webb, *Slaves, Women and Homosexuals: Exploring the Hermeneutics of Cultural Analysis* (Downers Grove, IL: InterVarsity Press, 2001).

9. Walter Brueggemann, *The Prophetic Imagination,* 2nd ed. (Minneapolis: Fortress, 2001), 21–38. While citing the usefulness of Brueggemann's dichotomy between "the prophetic imagination" and "the royal consciousness," I should also note that he appears to press the divide too far at points. The fact remains that God did sometimes

work through the royals to bring needed reforms, and to bless his people.

10. This would be a logical place to discuss the controversial subject of divinely sanctioned violence within the Old Testament. Unfortunately, time and space do not allow us to do justice to those questions here. For an introduction to the various questions and viewpoints, see the Counterpoints volume, edited by C. S. Cowles, *Show Them No Mercy: Four Views on God and Canaanite Genocide* (Grand Rapids, MI: Zondervan, 2003). For the absolute best book on the subject of love and violence within the world we *now* live in, see Miroslav Volf's masterpiece *Exclusion and Embrace: A Theological Exploration of Identity, Otherness, and Reconciliation* (Nashville: Abingdon Press, 1996).

11. For a biblical definition of "true religion," see James 1:27.

12. For further proof of God's opinion on Israel's wayward rulers, see Hosea 13:10–11.

13. In the (somewhat controversial) view of N. T. Wright, many Israelites believed that the exile would not truly be over until the nations gathered in Jerusalem to honor the name of the one true God. And for those eking out an impoverished existence under the boot of a foreign empire, it was clear that this had not yet happened. For a clear example of the Old Testament expectation, see Jeremiah 3:14–17.

Chapter Four

1. I believe that I first heard this analogy from C. S. Lewis.

2. For the definitive biography on Guevara's life (thick enough to prop open even the largest of household doors), see Jon Lee Anderson's, *Che Guevara: A Revolutionary Life* (New York: Grove Press, 1997). Unlike

some other works, Anderson's work highlights both the terrible flaws and the abiding appeal of this violent and committed character.

3. Most scholars agree that there is no difference between Mark's "kingdom of God" and Luke's "kingdom of heaven." Both refer to what it would look like for God's rule to be established in this world. In this sense, both refer to true communion coming back to the creation.

4. Adapted from Matthew 5:43–48. Apologies to my British and Scottish kin.

5. See Romans 5:12–15. Sadly, I cannot go into all of the biblically rooted models of atonement here. For an academic treatment of these themes, see my *Mosaic of Atonement: Toward an Integrated Icon of Christ's Work* (forthcoming).

6. In saying this, I have tried to set forth (simply) some of the basic models of atonement—all of which are found within the Scriptures.

   • *Recapitulation:* Christ reliving the human story successfully on our behalf, as the true Adam and true head of the human family.

   • *Penal Substitution:* Christ bearing the penalty for human sin in our place and instead of us. As I will argue, the basis for this action resides in Christ's identity as the true Adam. In the Bible, people are bound up with their King, or head. Hence in the Bible, the head may act on behalf of the whole.

   • *Moral Influence:* In his life and work, Christ shows us how we ought to live. And his example enflames our hearts with love for him by the power of the Holy Spirit.

   • *"Christus Victor" (Christ, the victor):* Finally, Christ's saving work is also depicted as a great triumph over sin, death, and the devil. It is, as we have said, a kind

of battle that is won in the most subversive way
imaginable: by a sacrificial death.

7. In John's gospel, the phrase comes to us in the Greek,
even while Latin was the official language of Rome. *Ecce
homo* is the wording used in Jerome's Latin translation
of the Scriptures.

8. John 19:5. For a brilliant (though dense) treatment of
Pilate's *Ecce homo,* see Dietrich Bonhoeffer's *Ethics,* ed.
Clifford J. Green, trans. Reinhard Krauss, Charles C.
West, and Douglas W. Stott (Minneapolis: Fortress,
2005), 82–92.

9. See Friedrich Nietzsche's, *On Reading and Writing.*

10. For more on the garden as the setting for Jesus' resurrection, and much more, see N. T. Wright's *The Resurrection
of the Son of God* (Minneapolis: Fortress, 2003).

11. For a compelling account for this kind of increased physi-
cality, see Wright, *The Resurrection of the Son of God,* 606.

12. See Wright, *The Resurrection of the Son of God,* 652.

13. This is the recurring line in Francis Spufford's
*Unapologetic: Why, Despite Everything, Christianity Can
Still Make Surprising Emotional Sense* (New York: Harper
One, 2013).

Chapter Five

1. To say that Christ's body is on earth may be a bit
confusing. After all, we have already said that his resurrected body ascended to the throne of heaven. This is
true. As we will see, the church—by virtue of Christ's
Spirit within us—becomes the tangible presence of
Jesus on planet Earth, even while he sits enthroned in
heaven.

2. One of the symbols of God's presence in the temple and
tabernacle had been the little flames upon the sacred
lampstands. Such tongues of flame (which harkened back

to the burning bush, among other things) signaled that God was present in the dwelling. Hence, the flames that appeared above his people in Acts 2 signaled precisely the same thing: these ordinary people had become the dwelling place of God's Spirit, even as they themselves— in all their ordinariness—had been made holy.

3. By distancing the tongues (or languages) of Acts 2 from the so-called "self-induced hysterics" of Christian cable, I am *not* claiming that Christians may never speak in tongues today. In my view, God's Spirit *continues* to work in miraculous ways, even now, just as it did in the New Testament. For a crucial passage on the use of tongues today, see Paul's words in 1 Corinthians: "I thank God that I speak in tongues more than all of you. But in the church, I would rather speak five intelligible words to instruct others than ten thousand words in a tongue" (4:18–19).

4. In the first-century Hellenistic culture, adult circumcision (something done to Jewish babies) was not only a painful and possibly dangerous endeavor, but also a cause of great social disdain among non-Jewish males.

5. For a fantastic look at how we know which commands are merely cultural versus transcultural (that is, unchanging), see William J. Webb, *Slaves, Women and Homosexuals: Exploring the Hermeneutics of Cultural Analysis* (Downers Grove, IL: IVP Academic, 2001).

6. I believe I first heard this analogy (regarding the boat) from N. T. Wright.

7. This inn, and the story that follow, are entirely fictional. The analogy of the unfinished play was taken originally from N. T. Wright and then greatly embellished. For the original story, see his *The New Testament and the People of God* (Minneapolis: Fortress, 1992), 140. Other details concerning the life and times of

Stratford's favorite son were garnered from Anthony
Burgess's biography, *Shakespeare* (New York: Barnes
and Noble Publishing, 2006).

8. In the words of James K. A. Smith, this process of faithful
improvising is true of all people, not least Christians
attempting to obey the Bible. "We act in the world more as
characters in a drama than as soldiers dutifully following
a command." *Imagining the Kingdom: How Worship Works*
(Grand Rapids: Baker Academic, 2013), 127.

Chapter Six

1. As we will note within this chapter, the Bible does not
give us a ton of (literal) information on the specific
nature of the afterlife. Hence, while I am quite certain
that this movie is fiction, it takes its place alongside
other fanciful portrayals of our final states. See, for
instance, C. S. Lewis, *The Great Divorce*.

2. Donald Miller conveyed this thought in a live talk that I
attended many years ago. The so-called "conflict theory"
was taken partly from the work of Robert McKee,
*Story: Substance, Structure, Style and the Principles of
Screenwriting* (New York: Harper Collins, 1997).

3. Since writing this, R.E.M. has released a critically
acclaimed album which may call into question this
"washed-up" remark. My apologies.

4. The 2011 update to the NIV now represents a more
literal (and I think better) rendering of the Greek. In so
doing, it encompasses the broader implications of what
Paul is talking about without denying the fact that we
too are being made new.

5. This is Paul's point in saying that we have been
saved by grace, through faith to do good works. See
Ephesians 2:8–10.

6. First Corinthians 15:20, 23–24 gives perhaps the clearest picture of how new creation begins in Jesus, continues in us, and awaits its final fulfillment in the future.

7. I do not choose this triad randomly—at least not completely. In the biblical accounts of new creation, we see precisely these sort of things: elements of what we call "nature," references to plentiful wine, and music that brings praise to God alone.

8. For scholarly support, see Michael J. Gorman, *Apostle of the Crucified Lord: A Theological Introduction to Paul and His Letters* (Grand Rapids: Eerdmans, 2004), 160–61; or watch the YouTube video (produced by Seedbed) in which Ben Witheringon III discusses the rapture and dispensationalism. https://www.youtube.com /watch?v=cg8lRGqtMHc.

9. See N. T. Wright, *Surprised by Hope: Rethinking Heaven, the Resurrection, and the Mission of the Church* (New York: Harper One, 2008), 132–33.

10. For instance, Revelation 14:9–11 paints a painful picture of what it will be like for those who choose allegiance to false kingdoms over allegiance to the kingdom of God.

11. See especially Matthew 25:31–46. Ironically, Jesus' story of the sheep and the goats is aimed pointedly at religious people who assume they are in.

12. When we set ourselves up as the final judge, we thereby break the first and most basic biblical commandment: "Thou shalt have no other gods before me" (see Deuteronomy 5:7).

13. At this point, think back specifically to chapters 4 and 5. Both Jesus and the early church incurred religious wrath by extending acceptance to those deemed to be outside the religious circle.

14. C. S. Lewis, *The Last Battle* (New York: Harper Trophy, 1984), 211.

Conclusion

1. Jann S. Wenner and Joe Levy eds., *The Rolling Stone Interviews* (New York: Back Bay Books, 2007), 51–52. The interviewer, in this case, was Jann S. Wenner.
2. Remember, no "apple" is ever mentioned in Genesis 3.
3. While I am quite certain that this "happened/happens" way of describing Genesis 3 is not unique to me, I cannot recall where I first heard it.
4. In a statement attributed to Karl Barth, one thing we learn through Christ is that it is as godlike to be lowly as to be exalted.
5. Hence the words of Christ in Acts 1:8: "But you will receive *power* when the Holy Spirit comes on you; and you will be my witnesses in Jerusalem, and in all Judea and Samaria, and to the ends of the earth" (emphasis added).
6. Rainer Maria Rilke, *Rilke's Book of Hours: Love Poems to God,* trans. Anita Barrows and Joanna Macy (New York: Riverhead Books, 1996), I, 17.